Get It Write

Developing Writing Skills for Correct and Logical English

Yasuhiro Ichikawa

Peter Serafin

KINSEIDO

Kinseido Publishing Co., Ltd.
3-21 Kanda Jimbo-cho, Chiyoda-ku,
Tokyo 101-0051, Japan

Copyright © 2006 by Yasuhiro Ichikawa
　　　　　　　　Peter Serafin

All rights reserved. No part of this publication may be reproduced, stored in a retrieval system, or transmitted, in any form or by any means, electronic, mechanical, photocopying, recording or otherwise, without the prior permission of the publisher.

Cover design: VOLTAGE
Text design:　parastyle inc.
Illustrations: Eri Ichikawa

はじめに

　近年、大学は学問研究を中心とする場から、教育を重視する場へと変わりつつある。いかに学生が知識だけではなく、さまざまな能力を身につけて社会へ出て行くことができるかが重視されてきている。特に英語はどのような職業に就いたとしても、必要不可欠であると認識されている。学生は大学に入学して、さらに英語を学習し続けなければならないし、教員も真の実力を付けるように指導しなければならない。

　しかしながら、学生の英語力は真の意味でコミュニケーションを行うためには不十分であることが多い。特に、ニュアンスの違いや、言葉の持っている意味合いなどを理解しないでただ単に日本語を英語に直してしまう学生をしばしば目にする。

　このテキストは英語を母語としない我々が英語を学習していく中で、よく間違ってしまう表現や、ニュアンスの違いを理解しないで使ってしまっている表現などを学習することを主な目的として作成された。英語の母語話者がどのような気持ちでいろいろな表現を使うかを理解することは英語を母語としない我々にとっては非常に難しいことである。だからこそ、さまざまな表現の使い方や、英文を書くときに注意しなければならないルールなどを理解し、応用できる能力をつける必要がある。

　本書はPassage、Practice、Common Errors、Further Studyで構成されている。Passageは各課で学習する言葉の使い方を示すものであり、そのニュアンスを文脈からくみ取ってもらいたい。Practiceは様々な表現の使い方を理解するために作成した。この設問はTOEIC、TOEFLなどの試験に対応できるようにしてある。Common Errorsはここで扱う表現の代表例についてニュアンスの違いや使い方の違いを解説したものである。アメリカ英語を中心として説明してあるが、細かなニュアンスを理解してもらうため、イギリス英語での違いなどにも考慮してまとめてある。また、この内容及びPracticeの多くはLongman Learner's Corpusに準拠したものである。Further Studyはパラグラフ・ライティング（これは日本人学習者が最も苦手としているものだと考える）の基本ルールを理解しながら、基本的なパラグラフ・ライティングを練習するようにまとめてある。巻末に切り取って提出できるTASK SHEETを用意してあるので活用していただきたい。

　それぞれの表現はできるだけアメリカ英語を中心としてまとめたが、世界ではアメリカ英語ばかりでなく、さまざまな英語が使われている。また細かなニュアンスの違いなどは個人レベルで違うこともある。筆者としてはできるだけ一般的な使い方を辞書・文法書などを参考にまとめてみた。足りない部分についてはぜひお使いになる先生方が補足して頂ければ幸いである。

　この教科書を作成するに当たって、Longman Learner's Corpusより用例を御提供いただいたLongman辞書部部長のDella Summers氏に深く感謝の意を表すものである。

編著者

Contents

Unit 1 **Making Friends at College** 1
Study Buddies
- 基本的な動詞の使い方 [1]
- パラグラフの基本

Unit 2 **My Frantic Day** 7
A Mad Dash to the Airport
- 基本的な動詞の使い方 [2]
- 時間軸でパラグラフを構成する

Unit 3 **Time Is Not Money** 13
Volunteer for Fun!
- 動詞＋名詞句の使い方 [1]
- 重要度の順でパラグラフを構成する

Unit 4 **Tokyo Disney Resort** 19
Making the Distinction between Land and Sea
- 動詞＋名詞句の使い方 [2]
- 空間秩序でパラグラフを構成する

Unit 5 **Overseas Travel** 25
An Opportunity for Personal Growth
- 間違いやすい動詞の使い方 [1]
- メインアイディアを補う：個人的な経験を利用する

Unit 6 **Sugar Blamed for Increased Obesity Worldwide** 31
Too Much Sugar Makes People Fat
- 間違いやすい動詞の使い方 [2]
- メインアイディアを補う：事実と引用を利用する

Unit 7　**Making the Perfect Cup of Coffee**　　　　　37
Brew It Right
- 間違いやすい名詞の使い方 [1]
- 指示を与えるパラグラフの書き方：過程と順序を知る

Unit 8　**The Statue of Liberty**　　　　　43
Welcoming Visitors for Over a Century
- 間違いやすい名詞の使い方 [2]
- 描写をするパラグラフの書き方：人や物を描写する

Unit 9　**Opinion**　　　　　49
Letter to a Newspaper
- 間違いやすい形容詞の使い方 [1]
- 主張を述べるパラグラフの書き方：主張を述べ、展開する

Unit 10　**English Language Newspapers**　　　　　55
Different Papers, Different Styles
- 間違いやすい形容詞の使い方 [2]
- 比較と対照を使ったパラグラフの書き方

Unit 11　**Managing Stress**　　　　　61
Your Key to College Success
- 間違いやすい副詞の使い方
- 原因と結果についてのパラグラフの書き方

Unit 12　**Writing Personal and Business Letters**　　　　　67
Communicating on Paper
- その他の間違いやすい表現
- 私信とビジネス・レターの書き方

Unit 1　Making Friends at College

- 基本的な動詞の使い方 [1]
- パラグラフの基本

Study Buddies

Passage　太字の語に注意しながら英文を読んでみましょう。

One of the most challenging aspects of college life is finding the right balance between social and academic activities. Everyone wants to have a good time with their friends, and get good grades, too. Fortunately, there is a way to have both. The answer is, make study buddies.

　A study buddy is a friend who studies at the same time as you do, and then plays when you do, too. The best study buddies are those who share common interests both in and outside of the classroom. For example, if you are **taking** an English class and you **like** movies, **ask** around to find a student in your English class whose hobby is going to movies. At the same time each week, you **meet** to study the material you are learning in class, and then after the work is done, **go see** a Hollywood movie together. This way you can kill two birds with one stone, learning the English you have to know for the test and then enjoying English in the form of entertainment.

　You will be amazed at how quickly the time passes and how fun the classes you **take** can be when you have someone to share the work with and a reward to look forward to afterwards. **Remember**, nothing is worse than **putting off** the work you have to do until it is too late. With regularly scheduled study buddy sessions, you will never have to worry. And in the end, it'll really pay off with your good grades, good friends, and good memories from the time spent in college.

Notes
grade [成績]　buddies > buddy [仲間]

Practice

A より適切な表現の英文にチェックをつけましょう。

1. ☐ We have to ask ourselves whether such films should be censored.
   ☐ We have to ask to ourselves whether such films should be censored.

2. ☐ The next morning she went to see us at the hotel.
   ☐ The next morning she came to see us at the hotel.

3. ☐ I don't like that my shoes get wet.
   ☐ I don't like my shoes getting wet.

4. ☐ He wants the new generation to keep up this tradition.
   ☐ He wants the new generation to keep on this tradition.

5. ☐ Whenever I go sightseeing, I take my camera with me.
   ☐ Whenever I go sightseeing, I bring my camera with me.

6. ☐ Would you please check whether I have forgotten a black handbag in Room 21?
   ☐ Would you please check whether I have left a black handbag in Room 21?

7. ☐ Since nobody would lend me the money, I ended up asking my father for it.
   ☐ Since nobody would lend me the money, I ended asking my father for it.

8. ☐ I can't wait to meet you again at Christmas.
   ☐ I can't wait to see you again at Christmas.

9. ☐ One of the men walked over to me and held my bag.
   ☐ One of the men walked over to me and took hold of my bag.

10. ☐ You'll have to fill in an application form.
    ☐ You'll have to fill an application form.

Unit 1　　Making Friends at College

B 誤りがあれば正しい英文に直しましょう。

1. The teacher told us to see what he was doing.

2. An ambulance arrived and the man was carried to the hospital.

3. The next time I met with her in the supermarket.

4. I would like to work at an international organization.

5. He told that he hadn't eaten anything for over a week.

6. We memorize seeing you at the station two years ago.

7. Kiri was always telling about herself and her problems.

8. Once indoors, he immediately put off his wet clothes and dried himself.

9. Even when she is angry, she never cries.

10. "Who paid the tickets?" I asked.

C 英語に直しましょう。

1. 彼らは彼に何をしたいと思っているのか尋ねました。

2. 日本から来ている学生はとても勤勉です。

3. あなたはその錠剤がなくなるまで飲み続けるべきです。

4. 彼はそこに午前中ずっと座って飛行機が離陸するのを見ていました。

5. 彼は道に迷い、家への戻り方がわからなくなった。

Common Errors ● 基本的な動詞の使い方 [1]

1.「連れて行く」「持って行く」のはbring、それともtake？

bringはcome with something/someoneという意味を持ち、takeはgo with something/someoneの意味を持っています。「別の方向へ何か／誰かと一緒に行く」場合はtake、「誰か／何かと一緒に自分のところへ来る（あるいは話し手のところへ行く）」場合はbringを用います。

ex. ●●●● Could you **bring** me a glass of water, please?
When I go on holiday, I like to **take** a good book with me.

2.「行く」はgoで「来る」がcome？

comeは通常「話し手のいる方向、または話にのぼっている人の方向へ行く」場合に用いられますが、goは「話し手の方向ではない、別の方向へ行く」場合に用いられます。母親に「ご飯だから来なさい！」と言われた場合、"I'm coming."と言えば、「今行きます」という意味になります。しかし、"I'm going."と言ってしまうと、母親の方向ではなく別の方向に行くことになり、「今出かけるところ」という意味になってしまいます。食事は片付けられてしまうでしょう。

3.「会う」はsee、それともmeet？

よく知っている人に挨拶をするとき、またよく知っている人に会う場合などは、meetではなくseeを使います。seeはまた、お互いが愛し合っていていつも会っているという場合などにmeeting someoneの意味で使います。meetは同じ場所でたまたま出会って話し始めたときや、意図的に出会ったときなどに用います。

ex. ●●●● I have **met** you here before.
I hope you'll come and **see** us again soon.

4.「つかむ」はholdではない？

holdは「手で何かを持つ／運ぶ」という意味を持っています。この場合、手や腕は持つための支えとして使われています。「手でつかむ」という場合はget hold ofを用います。get hold ofはput your fingers or hands around something and hold itという意味を表します。getの他にtakeも使われます。

ex. ●●●● Mother **took hold of** the barking dogs.

5.「見る」はsee、それともwatch、look？

seeは自分の視界の範囲に何かがあって「見える」とか「気づく」という意味を示します。一方watchは目を使い注意を払って見ている場合に使われます。lookは目的語をとれない自動詞なので、見つめる先をatで示します。

ex. ●●●● Did you **see** anyone go out?
After dinner we usually sit down and **watch** the news.
She **looked** at the people around her.

6. 「忘れる」はすべてforget？

leaveは持って来るはずのものをある場所に忘れた場合などに用いますが、forgetは持って来るということ自体が記憶からなくなってしまっていることを示します。

ex. If the keys aren't in your jacket, you must have **left** them in the restaurant.
Sorry to disturb you — I **forgot** my key.

7. 「着る」はput on、でも「脱ぐ」は？

put onは「着る」という意味ですが、その逆の「脱ぐ」はput offではありません。put offは「延期する」という意味になります。「脱ぐ」はtake offを用います。

ex. You have to **put on** your uniform now.
Don't **put** it **off** until tomorrow.

8. 「覚えている」はmemorize、それともremember？

「覚えている」という意味を表す単語はrememberです。memorizeは「暗記する、記憶する」という意味を表します。

ex. He studied his map, trying to **memorize** the way to Rose's street.
I **remember** seeing you here several years ago.

9. 「運ぶ」のはcarry、それともtake？

もし手に何かを持ってどこかへ行く場合、それを持って行くという意味でcarryを用います。一方誰かをどこかの場所へ連れて行く場合は、carryは使わずにtakeを使います。

ex. In some countries women **carry** their babies on their backs.
If you need a lift to the station, ask Peter to **take** you.

10. 「最終的に…で終わる」と言うときはendを使う？

endは通常自動詞として使われます。他動詞として使う場合には「…をとめる、終わらせる」という意味になります。一方、「最終的に…になる、…で終わる」という表現にはend up -ingを用います。

ex. The war **ended** in 1975.
To **end** the meal we had some coffee and an ice cream.
She **ended up telling** her husband everything.

Further Study　●パラグラフの基本

英語でのライティングはパラグラフが重要です。しっかりとしたパラグラフを作って自分の表現したい内容を伝えようとすることが、効果的なライティング（effective writing）につながります。

パラグラフは通常話題となることを示す文（topic sentence）で始まり、そのあとに、話題となっている内容を細かく述べたり支持したりする文が続きます。これらをsupporting sentencesと呼びます。最後に結論となる文（concluding sentence）を加えることが時々あります。

以下の文では、冒頭の文が話題（topic）となっていて、そのあとの文はその話題についての詳細な説明となっています。このような形が英文では一般的なので身に付けておく必要があります。

Topic Sentence	One of the most challenging aspects of college life is finding the right balance between social and academic activities. Everyone wants to have a good time with their friends, and get good grades, too. Fortunately, there is a way to have both. The answer is, make study buddies.
Supporting Sentences	A study buddy is a friend who studies at the same time as you do, and then plays when you do, too. The best study buddies are those who share common interests both in and outside of the classroom. For example, if you are taking an English class and you like movies, ask around to find a student in your English class whose hobby is going to movies. At the same time each week, you meet to study the material you are learning in class, and then after the work is done, go see a Hollywood movie together. This way you can kill two birds with one stone, learning the English you have to know for the test and then enjoying English in the form of entertainment. 　You will be amazed at how quickly the time passes and how fun the classes you take can be when you have someone to share the work with and a reward to look forward to afterwards. Remember, nothing is worse than putting off the work you have to do until it is too late. With regularly scheduled study buddy sessions, you will never have to worry. And in the end, it'll really pay off with your good grades, good friends, and good memories from the time spent in college.

Exercise

A 次のtopic sentencesからトピックを1つ選び、supporting sentencesを73ページのシートを使ってリストにしてみましょう。

- Exercise is necessary for good health.
- It is very important for parents to teach their children about ＊＊＊.
- ＊＊＊ is a good place to visit.

B 上のリストを利用してパラグラフを73ページのシートに書いてみましょう。

Unit 2 — My Frantic Day

- 基本的な動詞の使い方［2］
- 時間軸でパラグラフを構成する

A Mad Dash to the Airport

Passage 太字の語に注意しながら英文を読んでみましょう。

Yesterday was the most frantic day of my life. Let me tell you why.

Last summer my sister Keiko and her husband Steve, who live in San Francisco, visited Japan. They announced they were having a baby and Keiko asked me to come for the birth. I circled her due date on the calendar to **remind** myself and planned my trip.

Then yesterday morning, I was on a break between classes when my cell phone rang. It was Steve. "Megumi, the doctor says the baby is coming two weeks early. Keiko really wants you here with her. Can you **leave** right away — please?"

I said I would do my best. After all, my sister was about to **become** a mother.

First, I had to **call** the airline and change my ticket. There were no seats available, but they put me on standby and told me to come to the airport and **hope** for the best. Second, I had to **speak** to my professors and get out of classes before I could go.

I wasn't packed, so next I had to run home and throw some clothes into my suitcase. One of the wheels was broken and I couldn't carry it to the train station, so I had to **catch** a taxi.

Just as I got to the terminal I heard them paging my name. I ran to the ticket counter to **speak** to the agent. They had a seat!

Finally, I got on the plane, sat down and had a chance to **think**. What would Keiko's baby look like? What would he/she **grow up** to be? I **hope** I'll do a good job as Aunt Megumi.

Notes
frantic［大あわての］　mad dash［大あわてで向かうこと］　due date［予定日］
put ... on standby［…を待機させる］　paging > page［(名前を)呼び出す］

Practice

A より適切な表現の英文にチェックをつけましょう。

1. ☐ Please call me on 0248 312689.
   ☐ Please call me with number 0248 312689.

2. ☐ I ran downstairs to know what was happening.
   ☐ I ran downstairs to find out what was happening.

3. ☐ I was thinking if you would like to have lunch before visiting the museum.
   ☐ I was wondering if you would like to have lunch before visiting the museum.

4. ☐ He feels that they have made a big mistake.
   ☐ He is feeling that they have made a big mistake.

5. ☐ My company takes one of us to Singapore every six months.
   ☐ My company sends one of us to Singapore every six months.

6. ☐ Many of these children grow up in an atmosphere of violence.
   ☐ Many of these children grow in an atmosphere of violence.

7. ☐ Meanwhile, Sarah was beginning to be upset.
   ☐ Meanwhile, Sarah was beginning to become upset.

8. ☐ Ken's aunt left to New York on April 17th.
   ☐ Ken's aunt left for New York on April 17th.

9. ☐ The flowers reminded him his garden.
   ☐ The flowers reminded him of his garden.

10. ☐ I hope you have a good time at the party.
    ☐ I hope you to have a good time at the party.

Unit 2 My Frantic Day

B 誤りがあれば正しい英文に直しましょう。

1. The family broke just after he was born.

2. We hadn't seen each other for a year and so we spent the whole night speaking.

3. I got off my car to inspect the damage.

4. He cut the strip of photographs and gave one to me.

5. Looking through the magazine, I found out several interesting articles.

6. I didn't want to talk with him because I was in a hurry.

7. The dialogue in this video is very difficult to catch.

8. Then I looked the person sitting next to her.

9. When he arrived, they said him that his friend had died.

10. John said, "This old clock doesn't move."

C 英語に直しましょう。

1. 医者は彼のどこが悪いのかについての情報を得ようとしました。

2. 私は間違った駅で列車を降りました。

3. 警察は中に入るためにドアを壊さなければならなかった。

4. もしこのメモを受け取ったら、私に電話をしてください。

5. 私たちはなぜ人々がこんなひどいことをするのか考えるのにもっと時間を費やすべきです。

Common Errors ● 基本的な動詞の使い方 [2]

1.「…になる」はbecome、それともcome to？

becomeは"start to be"という意味で、状態の変化について述べるときに用います。becomeのあとには形容詞か名詞がきます。動詞があとに続く場合はcome to ...の形となります。

ex. In 1975 she **became** leader of the Conservative Party.
Eventually I **came to** like Singapore.

2.「情報を得る」のはfind、それともfind out？

findは偶然何かを見つけたり、探していて見つかったりするときに用います。一方、find outは「知りたいと思っていることに関しての情報を得る」という意味で用いられます。

ex. "I can't **find** my comb. Have you seen it anywhere?"
He's gone to **find out** which gate the plane leaves from.

3.「降りる」という場合、乗り物によって使う前置詞が異なってくる。

バスや電車、飛行機、船などから降りる場合はget offを用いますが、車やタクシーなどから降りる場合はget out ofを用います。「乗る」場合も、バス、電車などはget onを用い、車、タクシーなどはget intoを用います。

ex. The bus driver will tell you where to **get off**.
She **got into** a taxi.

4.「大きくなる」はgrow、それともgrow up？

自然のプロセスとして発達したり大きくなったりする場合はgrowを用いますが、子どもから大人へ成長していく場合はgrow upを用います。

ex. Mary's little boy **grew** four centimeters last year.
Of course I know him — we **grew up** together in New York.

5.「…かなと思う」はthink、それともwonder？

「…していただけないかしら、…なさいませんでしょうか」というような丁寧な依頼や招待を表す場合はwonderを用います。形はbe wondering if ...となり、thinkは用いません。

ex. I was **wondering** if you'd like to play tennis on Saturday.

6. 「出発する」の意味のleaveに付く前置詞はfor、to、それともfrom？

leaveを「…へ出発する」の意味で用いる場合、目的地はfor ...となります。出発地点は通常leaveの直後に（目的語として）置きますが、旅行などの始まる場所を特に述べたいときにはfrom ...を使うこともあります。

　　　　ex. ●●●●　　She'll be **leaving** (Tokyo) **for** London at nine o'clock.
　　　　　　　　　　　The coach will be **leaving from** in front of the hotel at six o'clock sharp.

7. thinkの場合の間接疑問とknowの場合の間接疑問とでは疑問詞の位置が違う。

do you knowやdo you thinkを用いた間接疑問文の疑問詞は、knowの場合は動詞の後ろに、thinkの場合は文頭に生じます。

　　　　ex. ●●●●　　Do you **know** who he is?
　　　　　　　　　　　Who do you **think** he is?

8. 「…と思う、…という感じを受ける」の場合は進行形にならない。

「…と思う、…という感じを受ける」などのように状態を表す表現は進行形にはなりません。このグループに入る動詞には、need、want、feel、love、like、thinkなどがあります。

9. breakはあとにくるものによっていろいろな意味になる。

breakは「壊す」という意味ですが、あとにくる要素とともに熟語表現を形づくるとさまざまな意味を示します。例えば、break up = stop being together as a couple or group、break down = separate something into smaller parts、break in = get into a building by forceなどがあります。

10. 「思い出させる」のはremember、それともremind？

remindは「cause + 人 + to remember ...」の意味で使われます。この動詞の後ろは「人 + of + 物事」という語句のつながりになることに注意しましょう。

　　　　ex. ●●●●　　This **reminds** me **of** Christmas parties.

Further Study ● 時間軸でパラグラフを構成する

しっかりとしたパラグラフの構成がgood writingの鍵となります。話題について文の内容を細かく述べていく場合、よく使われる手法の1つは時間の経過に基づいてイベントを構成するというものです。その中でよく使われる語彙としてはfirst、second、then、next、before、after、as、later、finallyなどがあります。また時を示す前置詞を使い、時間の流れに沿ってイベントを記述することもあります。

ここではfirst、second、finallyという語を用い、時間の流れに沿って内容を説明しています。また、thenがあることによって時間的に前の内容よりもあとに生じた事柄が書かれていることを示しています。

Topic Sentence	Yesterday was the most frantic day of my life. Let me tell you why.
Supporting Sentences	Last summer my sister Keiko and her husband Steve, who live in San Francisco, visited Japan. They announced they were having a baby and Keiko asked me to come for the birth. I circled her due date on the calendar to remind myself and planned my trip. **Then** yesterday morning, I was on a break between classes when my cell phone rang. It was Steve. "Megumi, the doctor says the baby is coming two weeks early. Keiko really wants you here with her. Can you leave right away — please?" I said I would do my best. After all, my sister was about to become a mother. **First**, I had to call the airline and change my ticket. There were no seats available, but they put me on standby and told me to come to the airport and hope for the best. **Second**, I had to speak to my professors and get out of classes before I could go. I wasn't packed, so next I had to run home and throw some clothes into my suitcase. One of the wheels was broken and I couldn't carry it to the train station, so I had to catch a taxi. Just as I got to the terminal I heard them paging my name. I ran to the ticket counter to speak to the agent. They had a seat! **Finally**, I got on the plane, sat down and had a chance to think. What would Keiko's baby look like? What would he/she grow up to be? I hope I'll do a good job as Aunt Megumi.

Exercise

● 次の指示に従って75ページのスケジュールを参考にしTime Orderに基づいたパラグラフを75ページのシートに書いてみましょう。

Mr. Kawakami is the director of an English Language School. Study his schedule for Wednesday, July 23. Write a paragraph about his day. Remember to begin with a topic sentence. Use signal words to guide the reader.

Unit 3 Time Is Not Money

- 動詞＋名詞句の使い方 [1]
- 重要度の順でパラグラフを構成する

Volunteer for Fun!

Passage
太字の語に注意しながら英文を読んでみましょう。

Do you know the expression "Time is money?" The traditional concept of work means trading the time you have for the money you need. One reason people go to college is to get a better paying job after graduation. A student's typical progression goes like this: First, decide what job to do in the future. Then, study a related major in college. Later, find the best paying job. Volunteer work, on the other hand, means giving your time away for free. According to the "Time is money" concept, volunteering is a waste of time. **Doing a job** for free may not seem logical, but volunteering is actually one of the best things you can do.

Each year college students from Japan volunteer for an exchange program at an elementary school in Hawaii. They spend two weeks teaching Japanese language and culture to the American children. After school the volunteers **do sports** with the kids. On the weekend, the host families **have a picnic** in the park or **go sightseeing**. The volunteers have many opportunities to use English and **improve their knowledge** of American culture. The program **has a positive effect** on everyone involved.

Because the volunteers are not professionals, they don't have to worry about **making a mistake** since they are not getting paid. They just **make an effort**, and feel free to **do some experiments**. As a result, everyone can **make progress** in a natural way, without worrying about the outcomes. When the volunteers look back on the great experiences they had, they realize there are other important things to do with one's time besides making money. And when they **have a job interview** they find that volunteering looks really good on the resume. Volunteering is a great way to **have fun** and **make a difference** at the same time.

Notes
trade［交換する］ typical progression［典型的な進み方］ volunteering［ボランティア活動］
get paid［給料をもらう］ resume［履歴書］

Practice

A より適切な表現の英文にチェックをつけましょう。

1. ☐ I always make a bath before going to bed.
   ☐ I always have a bath before going to bed.

2. ☐ We decided to make a picnic in the field opposite the house.
   ☐ We decided to have a picnic in the field opposite the house.

3. ☐ She took a positive attitude on this matter.
   ☐ She made a positive attitude on this matter.

4. ☐ Walking made a difference in his health.
   ☐ Walking had a difference in his health.

5. ☐ I've had six interviews but no one has offered me a job.
   ☐ I've made six interviews but no one has offered me a job.

6. ☐ We have made a great progress in the field of medicine.
   ☐ We have made great progress in the field of medicine.

7. ☐ I would like to get more knowledge during the course.
   ☐ I would like to improve my knowledge during the course.

8. ☐ I had an appointment with Takumi, a friend of mine.
   ☐ I had arranged to meet Takumi, a friend of mine.

9. ☐ I'm going to have a drink with some friends this evening.
   ☐ I'm going to take a drink with some friends this evening.

10. ☐ He does all types of sports.
    ☐ He makes all types of sports.

Unit 3   Time Is Not Money

B 誤りがあれば正しい英文に直しましょう。

1. I'm sure that you will get a lot of fun.

2. It happened a few years ago when I was making my university entrance exam.

3. There is no doubt that smoking gives an effect on people's health.

4. After lunch we went for sightseeing.

5. Mr. Barrett is going to get an operation on his back.

6. The government has made an agreement with the People's Republic of China.

7. He refuses to have sleeping pills.

8. It doesn't matter if you do a slight mistake.

9. The photographer made quite a good job.

10. Little effort has been done to investigate this claim.

C 英語に直しましょう。

1. 彼女はもっと柔軟な態度をとるべきです。

2. 先月、彼らは経営者と賃金契約を結びました。

3. 散歩が彼女の健康状態を大きく変えました。

4. 学生たちは実験が行われている間、じっと見守っていました。

5. 真理子は英語がすばらしく上達しました。

Common Errors ●動詞＋名詞句の使い方 [1]

1.「合意する」に用いる動詞はmake、それともreach？

「合意」は「する」のではなく、「達する」ものです。したがってmakeではなくreachを用います。またcome to / work out an agreementという表現もあります。

ex. ●●●● After a week of talks, Britain and Iceland **reached agreement** on fishing limits.
Recent government attempts to **work out an agreement** have proved unsuccessful.

2.「努力をする」に用いる動詞はmake、それともdo？

「努力」にはmakeを用い、doは用いません。

ex. ●●●● The manager would like to see the whole team **making more of an effort**.

3.「スポーツをする」に用いる動詞はdo、それともmake？

「スポーツをする」はdo sportあるいはplay sportsとします。doの場合、sportは不可算名詞であり不定冠詞のaは付きません。

ex. ●●●● Do you **do any sport** at school?
I have been an asthmatic from childhood and was never able to **play any sports**.

4.「態度をとる」に用いる動詞はmake、それともtake？

「態度をとる」はtake an attitudeとし、makeを用いることはありません。makeを用いるのはmake one's attitude clearのように「態度を明らかにする」という熟語表現の場合です。

ex. ●●●● She **takes a haughty attitude** to her inferiors.

5.「影響する」に用いる動詞はeffect、affect？

「影響する」という表現にはaffectを用います。effectは名詞でhave an effect on ...という形で用い、giveは用いません。

ex. ●●●● I thought that the long illness would **affect** my chances of passing the exam.
I thought that the long illness would **have an effect on** my chances of passing the exam.

6.「知識を身に付ける」に用いる動詞はget、それともimprove？

「知識を身に付ける」はgetではなく、improve/increase/brush up one's knowledgeという表現を用います。

    ex. ●●●●   I'd like to **improve my knowledge** of Asian cultures.

7.「飲む」の場合は、飲むものによって用いる動詞が違ってくる。

「お酒」を飲む場合はhave a drink、「コーヒー」の場合はhave coffee、「薬」を飲む場合はtake a medicine/drugなどと言います。同じ、「飲む」でも動詞が違うので注意しましょう。

    ex. ●●●●   Do not **have a drink** or **take drugs** to calm yourself down.

8.「進歩をする」のはひとつひとつ？

progressは不加算名詞（数えられない名詞）ですから、aを付けることはできません。また、「進歩がない」という表現はmake no progressと言うことができます。

    ex. ●●●●   He has **made great progress** in English since he came to the US.
                     They are **making no progress** in their efforts to resolve the crisis.

9.「実験をする」に用いる動詞はmake？

「実験」は「作る」ものではなく、「行う」ものです。したがって、makeではなく、perform、conduct、carry out、doなどを動詞として用います。

    ex. ●●●●   Further experiments will have to be **conducted/performed/carried out** before the drug can be tested on humans.

10.「観光に行く」に用いるのはgo -ing、それともgo for？

「観光に行く」はgo sightseeingであり、go for sightseeingではありません。go for ...となるものには、go for a walk、go for a hikeなどがあります。

    ex. ●●●●   If you **go sightseeing**, you travel around visiting the interesting places that tourists usually visit.

Further Study ● 重要度の順でパラグラフを構成する

情報の中身を構成していく2つ目の方法は重要性の順番にまとめていくことです。この場合、最も重要度の低い内容から始め、最も重要度の高いものへと論をすすめていくのが一般的です。その際よく使われるsignal wordsには、first、second、moreover、first of all、third、most importantly、for one thing、also、for example、in addition、the next …、another …、the most important …などがあります。

ここでは最初の文が話題(topic)となっていて、そのあとの文はその話題の詳細な説明として重要性の低い順番で説明を加えています。はっきりとfirst、second、third、the most important thingというように示すと書きやすいでしょう。

Topic Sentence: Do you know the expression "Time is money?" **The traditional concept of work means trading the time you have for the money you need.**

Supporting Sentences: One reason people go to college is to get a better paying job after graduation. A student's typical progression goes like this: **First**, decide what job to do in the future. **Then**, study a related major in college. **Later**, find the best paying job. Volunteer work, on the other hand, means giving your time away for free. According to the "Time is money" concept, volunteering is a waste of time. Doing a job for free may not seem logical, but volunteering is actually one of the best things you can do.

Each year college students from Japan volunteer for an exchange program at an elementary school in Hawaii. They spend two weeks teaching Japanese language and culture to the American children. After school the volunteers do sports with the kids. On the weekend, the host families have a picnic in the park or go sightseeing. The volunteers have many opportunities to use English and improve their knowledge of American culture. The program has a positive effect on everyone involved.

Because the volunteers are not professionals, they don't have to worry about making a mistake since they are not getting paid. They just make an effort, and feel free to do some experiments. As a result, everyone can make progress in a natural way, without worrying about the outcomes. When the volunteers look back on the great experiences they had, they realize there are other important things to do with one's time besides making money. And when they have a job interview they find that volunteering looks really good on the resume. Volunteering is a great way to have fun and make a difference at the same time.

Exercise

A 77ページのsupporting pointを重要度の度合いで番号をつけてみましょう。

B 上のリストを利用してそれぞれのtopic sentenceに続けてパラグラフをつくってみましょう。

Unit 4 Tokyo Disney Resort

- 動詞＋名詞句の使い方 [2]
- 空間秩序でパラグラフを構成する

Making the Distinction between Land and Sea

Passage 太字の語に注意しながら英文を読んでみましょう。

Tokyo Disney Resort is a huge complex consisting of two theme parks, a shopping mall and many resort hotels. The resort is so big it has its own monorail line. With so many places to go to and things to do, it is a fine location to **have a holiday**. But be forewarned, it is hard to **make a distinction** between some of the attractions without detailed maps.

From the nearest train station, Ikspiari Mall is on the left. A destination in itself, inside this swanky shopping complex are over a hundred stores and an array of restaurants where visitors can **have breakfast, lunch or dinner**. Toward the rear of the mall is a 16-screen movie theater, one of the largest in Japan. Adjacent to the mall you can catch the monorail and **make the journey** to the newest and furthest away portion of the resort, Disney Sea. Opened in 2001, this ocean-oriented theme park is one of a kind.

Those who **have experience** with Disneyland will find the Tokyo version similar to the original in Anaheim, California; except of course, that the Disney characters here speak Japanese. Like in California, Cinderella's Castle is in the center of the park, with Tomorrowland to the far right, Fantasyland at the rear, Adventureland to the far left, and the various other "lands" sandwiched in between.

Also, like at all Disney theme parks, it is forbidden to **hold a demonstration** or **make a speech** of any kind on the premises. If you **have a problem** at the park, staff members are ready to help. Should you **commit an offense** of some kind, you would be promptly apprehended by Disney security. On the surface, the Disney resorts **make an impression** of being all about dreams and imagination, but behind the scenes it's pure business.

Notes
complex [複合施設] forewarned > forewarn [警告する] swanky [しゃれた] ocean-oriented [海が中心となった]
premise [敷地] promptly [即刻] apprehended [逮捕する]

Practice

A より適切な表現の英文にチェックをつけましょう。

1. ☐ Every morning my first job is to prepare a breakfast.
   ☐ Every morning my first job is to prepare breakfast.

2. ☐ He wanted to make a good impression on his girlfriend.
   ☐ He wanted to make a good impression to his girlfriend.

3. ☐ She takes a vacation once in a blue moon.
   ☐ She makes a vacation once in a blue moon.

4. ☐ Harsh punishment would deter other students from doing the offense.
   ☐ Harsh punishment would deter other students from committing the offense.

5. ☐ Many demonstrations have been made in recent years in protest against the level of pollution.
   ☐ Many demonstrations have been held in recent years in protest against the level of pollution.

6. ☐ He kept telling the same joke again and again.
   ☐ He kept saying the same joke again and again.

7. ☐ I was invited to make a speech on the radio.
   ☐ I was invited to give a talk on the radio.

8. ☐ I've started to have lessons in English and French.
   ☐ I've started to get lessons in English and French.

9. ☐ It only takes me a minute to do a shower.
   ☐ It only takes me a minute to take a shower.

10. ☐ After taking the medicine, I felt sleepy.
    ☐ After drinking the medicine, I felt sleepy.

B 誤りがあれば正しい英文に直しましょう。

1. I made my first teaching experience in Scotland.

2. Next Saturday we're celebrating a small party at John's house.

3. Once one has taken the habit, smoking is very difficult to give up.

4. You should get on a taxi at the next station.

5. If you hold any complaints about the service, you should write to the manager.

6. They did a stormy argument yesterday.

7. You can't have a journey to Alaska without making careful preparations.

8. You can talk as long as you don't make a loud noise.

9. We usually take a tea with her in the afternoon.

10. I experienced problems to find the right accommodation.

C 英語に直しましょう。

1. ロンドンでは学生と講師らが提案されている教育費削減に反対する大規模なデモを行った。

2. 彼は爪をかむという癖がついてしまった。

3. 時に技能と経験をはっきりと区別することは難しい。

4. 彼はさまざまな軽い(minor)罪を犯したことで訴えられている(訴える=accuse of)。

5. もし道路が水浸しになっていたら船で旅行をしなければならないでしょう。

Common Errors ● 動詞＋名詞句の使い方 [2]

1.「印象を与える」に用いる動詞はgive、それともmake？

「印象を与える」の動詞にはgiveではなく、makeを用います。さらに、「…に印象を与える」での「…に」はtoではなく、onを用います。

> ex. ●●●● His first priority was to **make a favorable impression on** the prison warden.

2.「デモをする」の動詞にはmakeを用いない。

「デモをする」にはmakeではなく、holdもしくはstageを用います。

> ex. ●●●● In London, students and lecturers **staged a mass demonstration** against the proposed education cuts.

3.「朝食・昼食・夕食」は数えられるもの？

breakfast、lunch、dinnerなどは「食事」ではなく"event"としてとらえられるので、通常aは付きません。ただし、形容詞が加わると「食事」と見なされてaが付くことになります。

> ex. ●●●● Have you **had breakfast** yet?
> I **had a delicious lunch** yesterday.

4.「演説をする」に用いる動詞はgive、それともmake？

「演説をする」ではmake、giveの両方を用います。ここで用いるspeechは会議などで、政治家や重要な人物が行うものです。一方、情報を与えたり、講演者が行うような話をするという場合はgive a talkと言います。

> ex. ●●●● I heard her **make a very eloquent speech** at that dinner.
> He **gave** us such **an interesting talk** last year.

5.「習慣／癖がつく」に用いる動詞はtake、それともacquire？

「習慣／癖がつく」にはtakeではなく、acquireを用います。他の動詞では、adopt、develop、get intoなどを用います。

> ex. ●●●● Once one has **acquired the habit**, smoking is very difficult to give up.
> He's **developed the unfortunate habit** of biting his fingernails.

6. 「罪を犯す」に用いる動詞はcommit、それともdo？

「罪を犯す」という意味ではcommitという動詞を用います。commit a crimeという表現もあります。
　　　ex.　●●●●　He is accused of **committing various minor offenses**.

7. 「旅行をする」に用いる動詞はhave、それともmake？

「旅行をする」はmake a journey、あるいはgo on a journeyと言います。
　　　ex.　●●●●　He decided to **make a journey** through Europe.

8. 「経験する」に用いる動詞はmake、それともhave？

「経験する」はhave an experienceと言い、makeは用いません。「経験する」という意味では実際に経験する事柄を持つことになるので、experienceは数えられます。
　　　ex.　●●●●　The streets were full of beggars and we **had one or two very unpleasant experiences**.

9. 「薬を飲む」に用いる動詞はdrink、それともtake？

「薬を飲む」はtake the medicineもしくはhave the medicineと言い、drinkを用いません。また、「薬」にはmedicineのほかに「丸薬」pills、「錠剤」tablets、「粉薬」powdered medicine、「カプセル」capsules、「水薬」liquorなどがあります。
　　　ex.　●●●●　Have you **taken/had your medicine** today?

10. 「クレームをつける、不満がある」の動詞にはholdを用いる？

「クレームをつける、不満がある」はhold a complaintではなくmake a complaintと言います。また、「…に」にはtoではなくaboutを用います。
　　　ex.　●●●●　He **made a complaint** about the service to the manager.

Further Study ● 空間秩序でパラグラフを構成する

ある場所の記述をする場合、何が置かれているか説明するには空間順序（space order）を使います。一つには説明を始めるポイントを決め（例えば自分が入ってきたところ）、そこから時計回りの順序で説明をしていきます。また、別のやり方としては左から右へ、上から下へ、後ろから前へという順序があります。

ある場所についての説明には、signal wordとして場所を示す前置詞を用いた表現が使われます。例えば、at、in、next to、on the right、at the end、in back of、in front of、on top of、in the center、in the middle、between、on the left、under、overなどです。

Topic Sentence	Tokyo Disney Resort is a huge complex consisting of two theme parks, a shopping mall and many resort hotels. The resort is so big it has its own monorail line. With so many places to go to and things to do, it is a fine location to have a holiday. But be forewarned, it is hard to make a distinction between some of the attractions without detailed maps.
Supporting Sentences	**From the nearest train station**, Ikspiari Mall is **on the left**. A destination in itself, inside this swanky shopping complex are over a hundred stores and an array of restaurants where visitors can have breakfast, lunch or dinner. **Toward the rear of the mall** is a 16-screen movie theater, one of the largest in Japan. **Adjacent to** the mall you can catch the monorail and make the journey to the newest and furthest away portion of the resort, Disney Sea. Opened in 2001, this ocean-oriented theme park is one of a kind. Those who have experience with Disneyland will find the Tokyo version similar to the original in Anaheim, California; except of course, that the Disney characters here speak Japanese. Like in California, Cinderella's Castle is in the center of the park, with Tomorrowland to **the far right**, Fantasyland at the rear, Adventureland to **the far left**, and the various other "lands" sandwiched in between. Also, like at all Disney theme parks, it is forbidden to hold a demonstration or make a speech of any kind on the premises. If you have a problem at the park, staff members are ready to help. Should you commit an offense of some kind, you would be promptly apprehended by Disney security. On the surface, the Disney resorts make an impression of being all about dreams and imagination, but behind the scenes it's pure business.

Exercise

A 次の中から場所を1つ選び、79ページのシートにその絵を描いてみてください。そしてその場所を具体的に説明するための言葉をリストにしてみましょう。

- your favorite room in your house or apartment
- your favorite place to study
- your office or classroom

B 上のリストを利用して79ページのシートにパラグラフを書いてみましょう。

Unit 5 Overseas Travel

- 間違いやすい動詞の使い方 [1]
- メインアイディアを補う：個人的な経験を利用する

An Opportunity for Personal Growth

Passage
太字の語に注意しながら英文を読んでみましょう。

Many people consider vacations to be little more than a way to **pass** time and **amuse** themselves, but traveling abroad is actually an excellent way to learn about the world and discover one's true calling. I **realized** this through my personal experience of international travel after college.

After **obtaining** my college degree, I was **expected** to go right to work and begin my career. It wasn't easy to **convince** my family to **allow** me to take time off to travel overseas. They were afraid the trip would **interrupt** my career path and **prevent** me from getting a good job. But I was determined to see new places, so I booked an around-the-world ticket and set off on the journey that changed my life.

On my trip I met fellow travelers from all over the world. I found that I **enjoyed** communicating with people who spoke other languages and had different customs than my own. I explored strange cities, stayed in the homes of people in remote villages, and visited architectural wonders built by ancient civilizations. After all my experiences, I **realized** that I did not want to return to America and begin a conventional job in the place I grew up.

As a result, I sought a job in international journalism and was hired by an overseas bureau of a prominent newspaper. In my free time, and sometimes as part of my job, I am able to visit other countries. I found my true calling during my post-university trip. That's something I never would have discovered if I'd simply stayed home and done the conventional thing.

Notes
true calling［天職］　take time off［休みを取る］　fellow traveler［(旅の)道連れ］　conventional job［型にはまった仕事］

Practice

A より適切な表現の英文にチェックをつけましょう。

1. ☐ When I was a child, I used to raise my own flowers in a corner of the garden.
   ☐ When I was a child, I used to grow my own flowers in a corner of the garden.

2. ☐ We all tried to persuade her to sing.
   ☐ We all tried to convince her to sing.

3. ☐ Mr. Tong was appointed manager of the company in 1984.
   ☐ Mr. Tong was nominated manager of the company in 1984.

4. ☐ I made a lot of new friends during my stay in England and amused myself a lot.
   ☐ I made a lot of new friends during my stay in England and really enjoyed myself.

5. ☐ The public are demanding stricter laws.
   ☐ The public are claiming stricter laws.

6. ☐ In his last film he played a middle-aged school teacher.
   ☐ In his last film he performed a middle-aged school teacher.

7. ☐ I didn't join them on their walk because I didn't want to destroy my new shoes.
   ☐ I didn't join them on their walk because I didn't want to spoil my new shoes.

8. ☐ I was surprised that nobody wanted to inspect my luggage.
   ☐ I was surprised that nobody wanted to control my luggage.

9. ☐ The noise of the traffic disturbs the local residents.
   ☐ The noise of the traffic interrupts the local residents.

10. ☐ Finally we got really worried and alarmed the local police.
    ☐ Finally we got really worried and alerted the local police.

Unit 5　　　　Overseas Travel

B 誤りがあれば正しい英文に直しましょう。

1. I expect that you will be able to come to the party.

2. The government pretends to nationalize all the major industries.

3. A friend of mine has proposed me a job in his restaurant.

4. We can't accept a motorway to be built through our town.

5. I'm sure you will realize the song when you hear it.

6. Unemployment appears in nearly all developed countries.

7. It has taken women a long time to obtain equality.

8. These new measures are intended to avoid the spread of the disease.

9. We like to pass our holiday near the sea.

10. Some teachers neglect how much a student can take in during one lesson.

C 英語に直しましょう。

1. 私が次に彼女に会ったのはレストランでした。

2. 彼女は陪審 (jury) に自分の無実を納得させられなかった。

3. 彼らは彼が抜け出さないようにすべてのドアのかぎをかけた。

4. 家に帰る飛行機の中で私はホテルにコートを置き忘れたことに突然気づいた。

5. 彼の演説 (lecture) は聴衆に深い感銘を与えました。

Common Errors ● 間違いやすい動詞の使い方 [1]

1.「だめになる」はdestroy、それともspoil？

「何かが魅力がなくなったり使いにくくなった」または「ある事柄の楽しみがなくなった」などという場合の「だめになる」には、destroyではなくspoilまたはruinを用います。

ex. ●●●● This unpleasant man with his endless complaints **spoiled** my journey.

2.「楽しむ」はamuse、それともenjoy？

「退屈な状況から脱するために何かをして楽しむ」場合はamuse oneselfを使いますが、「楽しい時間を過ごして楽しむ」場合はenjoy oneselfを用います。

ex. ●●●● Can't you find something to do to **amuse yourself**?
The party was a huge success and all the guests **enjoyed themselves**.

3.「勧める」はpropose、それともoffer？

proposeは「正式にアイディアやプランを提案する、勧める」という場合に用いますが、offerは「相手が望むならやってあげられることを伝えてやる」場合や、「自分がしたいことを相手に話す」場合に用います。

ex. ●●●● May I **propose** that we postpone further discussion of this matter until our next meeting?
He **offered** to drive me back to my hotel.

4.「わかる」はrealize、それともrecognize？

realizeは「ある事実や、何かの本当の意味に突然気がついた」場合に用い、recognizeは「以前に見たり、聞いたりなどしたことがあって何であるかを知っている」場合などに用います。

ex. ●●●● I suddenly **realized** that the thumping I could hear was the sound of my own heart.
I'm sorry I didn't **realize** you — you've had your hair cut.

5.「じゃまをする」はinterrupt、それともdisturb？

interruptは「誰かが話をしていたり何かをしている時にその人の行動をやめさせる」場合に用います。一方、disturbは「誰かが今していることを続けるのを困難にさせる」場合に用います。

ex. ●●●● I'm sorry to **interrupt** but there's an urgent phone call for you.
I think we're **disturbing** Martin. Let's go and talk in your office.

Unit 5　Overseas Travel

6.「問題が生じる」のはappear、それともoccur？

appearは目に見えるように「現れる」という意味で用います。一方、occurは予定外の事柄が「起こる」という意味で使います。また、予定していたことが「起こる」場合はtake placeを用います。

ex.
- A minute later the manager **appeared** and asked what was wrong.
- The crash **occurred** just minutes after take-off.
- The interview **took place** on a Friday afternoon.

7.「忘れる」はneglect、それともforget？

neglectは特に仕事などでしっかりと面倒を見そこなった場合や、何かをしそこなった場合などに「怠る、放っておく」という意味で用います。一方、forgetは何かをはっきりと理解しそこなった場合に用います。

ex.
- The garden had been badly **neglected** and will require a lot of attention.
- Children tend to **forget** that their parents like to have fun too.

8.「指名する」はnominate、それともappoint？

nominateは選挙や選抜で誰かを推す場合に用います。一方、appointは誰かに仕事や身分を与えるときに用います。

ex.
- We need to **nominate** someone to take over from Harry as our new public relations officer.
- Mr. Wilks has been officially **appointed** as the society's new public relations officer.

9.「育てる」はraise、それともgrow？

raiseは特に食料として売るために農場で植物や野菜、動物などを育てる場合に用います。一方、growは楽しみとして庭などで植物や花、野菜などを育てる場合に用います。

ex.
- He grew up in Nebraska, where his parents **raised** chickens.
- This year I thought I'd try **growing** a few tomatoes.

10.「認める」はaccept、それともallow？

acceptは人のアドバイスや意見、示唆などを受け入れる場合に用います。一方、allowは誰かに何かをすることを許す場合に用います。

ex.
- I **accepted** her suggestion and agreed to see the doctor that evening.
- Many parents do not **allow/permit** their children to watch violent films.

Further Study　●メインアイディアを補う：個人的な経験を利用する

topic sentenceを具体的に説明する文（supporting sentences）には個人的な経験に基づいた内容もあります。実際に自分に起こった事実を述べ、経験したことから話題となっている事柄に説明を加えていく手法はよく用いられるものの一つです。

ここでは話題（topic）となっている事柄（... traveling abroad is actually an excellent way to learn about the world and discover one's true calling.）について自分が旅行で経験した事柄を述べることによってsupporting detailsを示しています。

Topic Sentence	Many people consider vacations to be little more than a way to pass time and amuse themselves, but traveling abroad is actually an excellent way to learn about the world and discover one's true calling. I realized this through my personal experience of international travel after college.
Supporting Sentences	After obtaining my college degree, I was expected to go right to work and begin my career. It wasn't easy to convince my family to allow me to take time off to travel overseas. They were afraid the trip would interrupt my career path and prevent me from getting a good job. But I was determined to see new places, so I booked an around-the-world ticket and set off on the journey that changed my life. On my trip I met fellow travelers from all over the world. I found that I enjoyed communicating with people who spoke other languages and had different customs than my own. I explored strange cities, stayed in the homes of people in remote villages, and visited architectural wonders built by ancient civilizations. After all my experiences, I realized that I did not want to return to America and begin a conventional job in the place I grew up. As a result, I sought a job in international journalism and was hired by an overseas bureau of a prominent newspaper. In my free time, and sometimes as part of my job, I am able to visit other countries. I found my true calling during my post-university trip. That's something I never would have discovered if I'd simply stayed home and did the conventional thing.

Exercise

A 次に記述してある事柄のうち1つを選び、そのことについての個人的な経験を81ページのリストにあげてみましょう。

- Sometimes hard work is not rewarded.
- Things often don't turn out the way you planned.

B 次に自分が選んだ事柄について、リストの内容を使って81ページのシートにパラグラフを書いてみましょう。

Unit 6: Sugar Blamed for Increased Obesity Worldwide

- 間違いやすい動詞の使い方 [2]
- メインアイディアを補う：事実と引用を利用する

Too Much Sugar Makes People Fat

Passage
太字の語に注意しながら英文を読んでみましょう。

The World Health Organization says the number of overweight people in the world is **increasing** rapidly, especially among the young. This is causing serious health problems and may even **decrease** a nation's life expectancy.

The WHO says over one billion people in the world are overweight, and 300 million of those are obese. The problem has become much worse in recent years. The number of obese Japanese 9-year-olds has tripled **compared with** 1990. Today 10% of Chinese children living in cities are obese and 65% of Americans are overweight.

Two main causes are too little exercise and too much sugar. Currently 10% of the British diet and 25% of the American diet comes from added sugar.

"If nothing is done … for the first time in 100 years, life expectancy will go down," said John Crebs of Britain's Food Standards Agency.

The problem is not limited to developed countries. "Many people in poor countries now **suffer from** cardiovascular disease, diabetes, certain cancers, obesity — these are no longer rich country problems," says Dr. Gro Harlem Brundtland, Director-General of WHO. "We **know** that foods high in saturated fats and sugars are unhealthy."

He also mentioned the "horrifying **increase**" in the number of soft drinks consumed in the developing world, as well as in the US. To **deal with** the problem, some American schools now **refuse** to provide unhealthy foods to students and help them **choose** healthy diets.

To **improve** the situation, the experts **remind** people to **reject** unhealthy food. They also recommend people run, bicycle, swim or do other exercise for 30 minutes, 3–5 times per week.

Notes
The World Health Organization = WHO［世界保健機構］　life expectancy［余命、寿命］　obese［太りすぎの］
diet［食事（規定食、朝・昼・夕食のこと）］　Food Standards Agency［英国食品基準局］　cardiovascular［心臓血管の］
diabetes［糖尿病］　Director-General［事務局長］

Practice

A より適切な表現の英文にチェックをつけましょう。

1. ☐ A balanced diet is accomplished by eating many different kinds of food.
   ☐ A balanced diet is achieved by eating many kinds of food.

2. ☐ After just two months he resigned and went to work for a smaller company.
   ☐ After just two months he retired and went to work for a smaller company.

3. ☐ We can improve the economic situation by working harder.
   ☐ We can increase the economic situation by working harder.

4. ☐ He refused their lifestyle and decided to seek a simpler alternative.
   ☐ He rejected their lifestyle and decided to seek a simpler alternative.

5. ☐ Some people choose marriage partners who are totally unsuitable.
   ☐ Some people elect marriage partners who are totally unsuitable.

6. ☐ The car was running too fast for me to see the number plate.
   ☐ The car was moving too fast for me to see the number plate.

7. ☐ Overpopulation doesn't stop these countries from developing.
   ☐ Overpopulation doesn't permit these countries to develop.

8. ☐ People living in the city were not touched by the famine.
   ☐ People living in the city were not affected by the famine.

9. ☐ The train was so full that I was frightened of getting squeezed.
   ☐ The train was so full that I was frightened of getting squashed.

10. ☐ May I remind you of what happened that day?
    ☐ May I recall you what happened that day?

B 誤りがあれば正しい英文に直しましょう。

1. Have you been in California?

2. I searched my passport everywhere but couldn't find it.

3. One of the bottles including the virus had been stolen.

4. The other passenger suffered from serious leg injuries.

5. The best way to know the city is to visit it on foot.

6. The play deals in the struggle of a married couple to live their own lives.

7. I would greatly appreciate if you could send me Ray's address.

8. We sat there watching the leaves falling down from the trees.

9. The teachers will visit our school and compare our teaching method to their own.

10. I'm doing the course to expand my job opportunities.

C 英語に直しましょう。

1. 私は友達をまねてそのクラブにも入ると思います。

2. 彼はナショナルチームの一員に選ばれました。

3. 子どものとき私たちはすべての人が食べ終わるまでテーブルを離れることを許されませんでした。

4. 彼女はジャーナリズムを通してもっと多くのことを成し遂げることができると感じました。

5. その休日旅行 (holiday package) にはライン川の2日間クルーズが含まれます。

Common Errors ● 間違いやすい動詞の使い方 [2]

1.「含む」はinclude、それともcontain？

includeは、含まれるものがそのパーツの一部になっている場合に用います。一方containは、箱やボトル、バッグなどの中に何が入っているかを言ったり、何かの中身を述べたりする場合に用います。

ex. The price **includes** a small charge for postage and packing.
The bag **contained** some old clothes.

2.「選ぶ」はchoose、elect、それともselect？

chooseは自分が望んでいるものを選ぶ場合に用い、electは選挙によって選出する場合に用います。一方、selectは最も適したもの、一番いいものを選択する場合に用います。

ex. We **chose** Greece because we hadn't been there before.
The committee has **elected** a new chairman.
They **select** books that seem important to them.

3.「成し遂げる」はaccomplish、それともachieve？

accomplishは満足のいくものをなんとか完成させた場合に用います。一方、achieveは計画していたことを（特に大変な努力をして）なんとかやり遂げた場合に用います。

ex. She felt that she could **accomplish** more through journalism.
The company intends to **achieve** all these goals within the next five years.

4.「広がる、増す」はexpand、increase、それともimprove？

expandはサイズや地域、活動が「広がる」という意味で用います。increaseは数や量、価格などが「大きくなる、増す」という意味で用います。一方、improveは「何かをよくする」、「何かがよくなる」という意味で用います。

ex. Within three years the business had **expanded** into a chain of department stores.
Sales of new cars **increased** from 1.2 million in 1993 to 1.8 million in 1994.
Efforts are being made to **improve** the quality of the medical services.

5.「辞める」のはretire、それともresign？

retireは、定年退職で職を去る場合に用います。resignは、自分がその仕事が好きではない場合や、もっとよい職が見つかって早期に退職する場合などに用います。一方、「クビになる」は、be dismissed、be firedなどと言います。

ex. In the UK, men usually **retire** at the age of 65 and women at 60.
If she doesn't get a salary increase, she's going to **resign**.
You are **fired**!

Unit 6　Sugar Blamed for Increased Obesity Worldwide

6.「苦しむ」はsuffer、それともsuffer from ?

sufferはけがや痛み、苦痛、損失などを「経験する、こうむる」という意味で用いますが、suffer fromは病気や飢餓、貧困などで「苦しむ」という意味で用います。

ex. 　　She can walk again, but she still **suffers** a lot of pain.
　　　　A lot of the children we saw were **suffering from** malnutrition.

7.「知る」はknow ?

knowは「知っている、知り合いである」という状態を表す動詞です。「知るようになる、知り合いになる」という意味では用いることができず、代わりにget to knowという表現を用います。また、「何かの情報を得る」という意味ではfind outを用います（Unit 2参照）。

ex. 　　I **know** Frankfurt very well.
　　　　We **got to know** each other very well during the week we spent together.

8.「断る」はrefuse、それともreject ?

refuseは、誰かがあなたにしてもらいたい、または受け入れてほしいと思っていることを「拒絶する」場合に用います。一方rejectは、あなたがアイディアや信念、プラン、提案などを「支持しない」という場合に用います。

ex. 　　Some of the staff **refuse** to attend lunchtime meetings.
　　　　Vegetarians **reject** the theory that you must eat meat to get all the nutrients you need.

9.「落ちる」はfall、それともfall down ?

fallは雨や雪、涙、葉などが自然に落ちていく場合に用いますが、fall downは自然に落ちていくのではなく、誤って落ちたりひざをついたりする場合や、何かが壊れる、失敗するなどの意味で用います。

ex. 　　The rain began to **fall** more heavily.
　　　　The house was cheap because it was **falling down**.
　　　　She **fell down** the stairs.

10.「押される」のはsqueeze、それともsquash ?

squeezeは、手で何かをしっかりと握る場合や果汁など何かをしぼる場合、また人や物を小さい空間に押し込む場合に用います。一方squashは、通常非常に強い力で壊してしまうほど何かを押さえつける場合に用います。

ex. 　　She **squeezed** my arm and told me not to worry.
　　　　Somehow we managed to **squeeze** everyone into the car.
　　　　"Be careful that you don't **squash** the tomatoes."

35

Further Study ● メインアイディアを補う：事実と引用を利用する

メインアイディア（トピック）を支持するためによく使われるものとして、事実や統計、引用などがあります。文章を上手に書く人はこれらを効果的に使います。

このパラグラフでは事実として統計上の資料をあげています。この資料によってメインアイディアが支持されています。統計だけではなく、引用文を支持証拠としてあげることもあります。この場合注意しなければならないのは、引用部分を引用符（クォーテーションマーク）で囲まなければならないことです。なお、引用した文章が疑問文である場合は、疑問符も引用符の中に入れなければなりません。

Topic Sentence

The World Health Organization says the number of overweight people in the world is increasing rapidly, especially among the young. This is causing serious health problems and may even decrease a nation's life expectancy.

Supporting Sentences

The WHO says over one billion people in the world are overweight, and 300,000 of those are obese. The problem has become much worse in recent years. The number of obese Japanese 9-year-olds has tripled compared with 1990. Today 10% of Chinese children living in cities are obese and 65% of Americans are overweight.

Two main causes are too little exercise and too much sugar. Currently 10% of the British diet and 25% of the American diet comes from added sugar.

"If nothing is done ... for the first time in 100 years, life expectancy will go down," said John Crebs of Britain's Food Standards Agency.

The problem is not limited to developed countries. **"Many people in poor countries now suffer from cardiovascular disease, diabetes, certain cancers, obesity — these are no longer rich country problems,"** says Dr. Gro Harlem Brundtland, Director-General of WHO. **"We know that foods high in saturated fats and sugars are unhealthy."**

He also mentioned the **"horrifying increase"** in the number of soft drinks consumed in the developing world, as well as in the US. To deal with the problem, some American schools now refuse to provide unhealthy foods to students and help them choose healthy diets.

To improve the situation, the experts remind people to reject unhealthy food. They also recommend people run, bicycle, swim or do other exercise for 30 minutes, 3–5 times per week.

Exercise

● 83ページの図を見て質問に答えてみましょう。

Unit 7: Making the Perfect Cup of Coffee

- 間違いやすい名詞の使い方 [1]
- 指示を与えるパラグラフの書き方：過程と順序を知る

Brew It Right

Passage
太字の語に注意しながら英文を読んでみましょう。

Making great coffee is a **skill** anyone can master. The drip method using a paper filter in a plastic or ceramic cone strikes the proper balance between flavor and convenience.

First, always buy whole coffee beans and store them in a tightly-closed jar. When you're taking a **break** from **homework** or **housework** and want some coffee, start by grinding the beans. Although some people use a hand-powered **machine**, an electric grinder is smaller, more convenient and works almost as well. Grind the beans for 45–60 seconds. If the grounds are too small, they'll stop up the filter and make the coffee bitter. If they are too large, the water will pass through too quickly to get the full flavor.

Next, place the filter into the coffee cone and add 20g of ground coffee for each 300ml cup. There is a direct **relationship** between the quality of the water and the taste of the coffee, so always use either bottled spring water or filtered water. Boil the water, then remove it from the heat and allow it to cool 60–120 seconds — until it reaches 95°C.

Then, place the cone on the cup and pour in the water. For best flavor, it should take 4.5–5 minutes for all the water to pass through the filter. Adjust the flow speed by experimenting with grinding time. When the coffee is brewed, immediately add sugar and/or fresh cream or milk if desired. Avoid "non-dairy creamers" that come in small packets as they can **damage** the flavor.

Finally, drink it quickly. Coffee maintains the perfect flavor for only about 10 minutes.

Notes
brew［(コーヒーを)入れる］ tightly-closed［しっかりと閉まった］ full flavor［豊かな風味］ spring water［わき水］

Practice

A より適切な表現の英文にチェックをつけましょう。

1. ☐ The police were grateful to the public for their collaboration.
   ☐ The police were grateful to the public for their cooperation.

2. ☐ The salary is 800 yen an hour.
   ☐ The wage is 800 yen an hour.

3. ☐ Between the first two classes there is a ten-minute break.
   ☐ Between the first two classes there is a ten-minute interruption.

4. ☐ He ran away from home after an argument with his father.
   ☐ He ran away from home after a discussion with his father.

5. ☐ Over eight percent of these cars are old, and so are their machines.
   ☐ Over eight percent of these cars are old, and so are their engines.

6. ☐ Although the film has its merits, it also has a serious flaw.
   ☐ Although the film has its advantages, it also has a serious flaw.

7. ☐ I decided to take a big stick with me, just as a precaution.
   ☐ I decided to take a big stick with me, just as a prevention.

8. ☐ My obligations include doing the housework and picking up the children from school.
   ☐ My duties include doing the housework and picking up the children from school.

9. ☐ The country shares boundaries with Rwanda and Burundi.
   ☐ The country shares borders with Rwanda and Burundi.

10. ☐ I wish to improve my speaking and listening skills.
    ☐ I wish to improve my speaking and listening capacities.

Unit 7　Making the Perfect Cup of Coffee

B　誤りがあれば正しい英文に直しましょう。

1. The other day I was given a gift certificate, but it was only worth two thousand yen.

2. It used to be difficult for women to get good occupations.

3. She claimed damage of $3,500 for wrongful dismissal.

4. In my opinion, women who go out to work don't have enough time to do the homework.

5. On almost every page there were announcements for cigarettes and tobacco.

6. There is not enough comprehension between our two countries.

7. There are so many unnecessary packages nowadays.

8. It's hard to tell which nations he comes from.

9. I thought that offering to help him might improve our relation.

10. Very few office workers get a good pay.

C　英語に直しましょう。

1. 彼女の車は大事故に巻き込まれました。

2. テレビは多くの利益を与えてくれます。

3. スキャンダルによって彼の政界での職は突然終わりを迎えた (bring ... to an end)。

4. 親は子供の欠点に気がつかないものです。

Common Errors ● 間違いやすい名詞の使い方 [1]

1.「利益」はadvantage、merit、それともbenefit？

advantageは他の人・物よりもよい立場にしてくれるものを表し、meritは人や物を賞賛に値するものとしてくれる「とてもよい長所」を示します。一方、benefitはその人の生活や状況を向上させてくれる「恩恵、特典」を表します。

ex. 　The main **advantage** of using a word processor is the amount of time you save.
　　 The **merits** of the new health program are gradually being recognized.
　　 It's over a month since I got back from holiday, but I still feel the **benefit**.

2.「クーポン」はcertificate、voucher、それともcoupon？

certificateはある人に関する事実が述べてある公的書類、つまり「証明書」を表します。voucherはお金の代わりに使うことのできるある種のチケット（金券）を表し、gift/luncheon/travel voucherなどのように用います。一方couponは、商品を割引したり無料にする券で、「割引券」「優待券」という意味を表します。

ex. 　Wives will have to bring along their marriage **certificate**.
　　 Take the **voucher** to your local branch of Woolworth's.

3.「仕事」はwork、job、occupation、それともcareer？

workは数えられない名詞として「仕事」の意味で用いたり、「働く場所」として用いたりもします。jobは生活をしていくための仕事を表したり、仕事のタイプを表したりします（a full-time job、a part-time jobなど）。jobとoccupationはほぼ同じ意味ですが、occupationのほうがformalな表現となります。一方、careerはworking life（勤労生活）を示したり、今まで働いてきた一連の職業（履歴）を表したりします。

ex. 　I got up and got ready to go to **work**.
　　 I know she works for the BBC but I'm not sure what **job** she does.

4.「給料」はsalary、wage、それともpay？

salaryは1年間の仕事に対して支払われるお金を示し、通常毎月銀行口座に支払われるものを表します。wageは例えば、週給、日給のようなもので、直接現金で支払われるものです。一方、payは人が行った仕事に対して支払われるお金のことを表し、数えられない名詞として扱います。

ex. 　She's on a **salary** of $50,000 a year.
　　 They've been given a **pay** raise (rise) of $40 a week.

5.「機械」はmachine、machinery、それともengine？

machineは有効な仕事をする装置の一部であり、a washing machine、a sewing machineなどのように用いることもあります。machineは数えられる名詞として扱います。machineryは「機械」全般を表す単語で、数えられません。engineは、自動車や飛行機などにパワーを供給する装置のことです。

ex. 　To operate this **machine**, select the type of coffee and press the button.
　　 In the distance I could hear the chug of farm **machinery**.

Unit 7　Making the Perfect Cup of Coffee

6. damageは数えられる、それとも数えられない？

damageは「損害、被害」などという意味では数えられない名詞として扱います。damagesという複数形の場合は「損害賠償額」あるいは「被害総額」という意味になります。

ex. ●●●●　The ceiling had suffered a great deal of **damage**.
　　　　　　She was awarded $30,000 in **damages**.

7.「議論」はargument、それともdiscussion？

argumentは「口げんか(quarrel)」あるいは「口論、言い争い」という意味を示します。一方discussionは何かについての話し合いで、お互いに意見を述べ合うようなもの、つまり「議論」という意味を示します。

ex. ●●●●　The couple next door are always having **arguments**.
　　　　　　After further **discussion**, the government has decided to reject the offer.

8.「理解」はcomprehension、それともunderstanding？

comprehensionは話されたり書かれたりした事柄の意味を理解する能力を示すものですが、understandingは共感・同情の姿勢を示す場合に用いられます。

ex. ●●●●　I'd like to develop my vocabulary and improve my listening **comprehension**.
　　　　　　When it comes to the employee's personal problems, the management shows a complete lack of **understanding**.

9.「休憩」はinterruption、それともbreak？

interruptionは、人が行っていたり話したりしていることを突然やめさせることを表します(「中断、妨害」)。一方breakは、生徒や労働者が自分のしたいことを行っているときに短期間、していることから解放されることを表します(つまり「休憩」)。

ex. ●●●●　To avoid further **interruption**, we locked the office door.
　　　　　　During their **break** the boys usually kick a ball around in the playground.

10.「協同、協調性」はcollaboration、それともcooperation？

collaborationは動詞のcollaborateから派生した名詞で、同じ仕事―特に科学・芸術・産業などの分野―を誰かと共同で行うことを表します。一方cooperationは動詞のcooperateから派生した名詞で、誰かが何かを達成する手助けをすることを表します。したがってcooperationが「協同、協調性」という意味を表します。

ex. ●●●●　Scientists hope the work done in **collaboration** with other researchers may be duplicated elsewhere.
　　　　　　We emphasized that his **cooperation** was important.

Further Study ●指示を与えるパラグラフの書き方：過程と順序を知る

何かをしたり、つくったりする方法を順を追って説明するときは、よく指示を与えます。指示する場合によく使われる方法としては、時間的順序に沿ってやり方を示したり（つまり、time orderを用いたり）、空間的順序に沿って教えたりします。いずれにせよ、指示を与える場合は、はっきりと、相手がついてこれるようにわかりやすく示さなければいけません。

ここでは最初の文が話題（topic）となっていて、そのあとの文は時間的順序（time orderに沿って）具体的な説明が加えられています。簡潔に示している点に注意しましょう。

Topic Sentence	**Making great coffee is a skill anyone can master.** The drip method using a paper filter in a plastic or ceramic cone strikes the proper balance between flavor and convenience.
Instructions	**First**, always buy whole coffee beans and store them in a tightly-closed jar. When you're taking a break from homework or housework and want some coffee, start by grinding the beans. Although some people use a hand-powered machine, an electric grinder is smaller, more convenient and works almost as well. Grind the beans for 45–60 seconds. If the grounds are too small, they'll stop up the filter and make the coffee bitter. If they are too large, the water will pass through too quickly to get the full flavor. **Next**, place the filter into the coffee cone and add 20g of ground coffee for each 300ml cup. There is a direct relationship between the quality of the water and the taste of the coffee, so always use either bottled spring water or filtered water. Boil the water, then remove it from the heat and allow it to cool 60–120 seconds — until it reaches 95°C. **Then**, place the cone on the cup and pour in the water. For best flavor, it should take 4.5–5 minutes for all the water to pass through the filter. Adjust the flow speed by experimenting with grinding time. When the coffee is brewed, immediately add sugar and/or fresh cream or milk if desired. Avoid "non-dairy creamers" that come in small packets as they can damage the flavor. **Finally**, drink it quickly. Coffee maintains the perfect flavor for only about 10 minutes.

Exercise

A 次のtopic sentencesからトピックを1つ選び、内容を構成する文を85ページのシートにあげてみましょう。

- plan a party
- study for an exam
- make your favorite dish

B 上のリストを利用してパラグラフを書いてみましょう。

Unit 8 The Statue of Liberty

- 間違いやすい名詞の使い方 [2]
- 描写をするパラグラフの書き方：人や物を描写する

Welcoming Visitors for Over a Century

Passage
太字の語に注意しながら英文を読んでみましょう。

I will always remember my first **impression** of the Statue of Liberty. I was a **stranger** riding on the ferry across New York Harbor, enjoying the urban **landscape** and skyline. I remember how small the statue looked in the distance.

"Lady Liberty" is one of the most recognized statues in the world, and is a great American symbol. She is a 151-foot copper statue of a woman in classical Roman **costume**. Her upraised right hand holds the "torch of liberty," and her left hand holds a book with the date July 4, 1776 — America's Independence Day. Upon her head is the "crown of liberty," with seven spikes representing the seven continents. The chains under her feet represent liberty crushing the chains of slavery. The statue was a gift of international friendship from the people of France in 1886 to celebrate American's 100th birthday. It is now a World Heritage Site.

The ferry to Liberty Island requires a **payment** of ten dollars, but admission to the Statue of Liberty itself is free. You can visit the Statue of Liberty museum at the base of the statue. There you can view the original torch, which was replaced in 1984. Visitors used to be able to climb a staircase in the statue to the crown. This was a favorite place for **photographers**, but was closed after the terrorist attacks of September 11th.

Over the past 120 years, countless people have sailed past Lady Liberty as they entered New York Harbor. The statue may have looked small to me the first time I saw her, but over the years she has been big enough to hold the dreams of millions of **foreigners** who came to start new lives in America.

Notes
torch of liberty ［自由の灯火］　Independence Day ［独立記念日］　spike ［角］

Practice

A より適切な表現の英文にチェックをつけましょう。

1. ☐ It is a custom in Japan to take off your shoes before entering a house.
   ☐ It is a habit in Japan to take off your shoes before entering a house.

2. ☐ My immediate ambition is to find somewhere to live.
   ☐ My immediate aim is to find somewhere to live.

3. ☐ The priest stands in front of the bride and groom, facing the audience.
   ☐ The priest stands in front of the bride and groom, facing the congregation.

4. ☐ The scholarship provided me with my first opportunity to travel overseas.
   ☐ The scholarship provided me with my first occasion to travel overseas.

5. ☐ Many kings chose to live here because of the beautiful landscape.
   ☐ Many kings chose to live here because of the beautiful scenery.

6. ☐ I decided to change my image and had my hair cut short.
   ☐ I decided to change my impression and had my hair cut short.

7. ☐ The price of keeping a person in prison for a year is enormous.
   ☐ The cost of keeping a person in prison for a year is enormous.

8. ☐ Tourism is the main source of money for these people.
   ☐ Tourism is the main resource of money for these people.

9. ☐ There are a lot of strangers visiting England.
   ☐ There are a lot of foreigners visiting England.

10. ☐ The main cause of unemployment is modern technique.
    ☐ The main cause of unemployment is modern technology.

B 誤りがあれば正しい英文に直しましょう。

1. Japanese manner is based on the idea that 'you are superior to me.'

2. Shotaro Akiyama is a famous Japanese cameraman.

3. The dancers were dressed in their national clothes.

4. We'll have to find new methods of amusing ourselves.

5. I was very nervous during the appointment so they may give the job to someone else.

6. In my new job I have to make a lot of important choices.

7. The cause why I want to change my job is as follows.

8. From the window, there was a beautiful scene of the lake.

9. Dr. Schneider charges a high payment but he is very good.

10. The main reason of the trip is to see Helen's parents.

C 英語に直しましょう。

1. 私は習熟度テスト(proficiency examination)を受ける機会がまったくありませんでした。

2. 彼はガールフレンドに良い印象を与えたかった。

3. 喫煙が肺がんの主な原因のひとつです。

4. ウエイターは請求書には10パーセントのサービス料金が含まれますと説明しました。

5. 先端技術には大規模な投資が必要です。

Common Errors ● 間違いやすい名詞の使い方 [2]

1.「支払い」はpayment、fee、price、それともcost？

paymentは何かに支払われるお金のことを示し、feeは医者や弁護士、その他専門職に就いている人へ支払われるお金(「料金」)のことを示します。一方priceは何かを買うために支払うお金(「値段」)のことを示し、costは何かを買ったり、したり、使うために支払うお金(「費用」)のことを示します。

ex. I had to get rid of the car because I couldn't keep up the **payments**.
The **fee** for a one hour private lesson is $60.

2.「目標」はambition、それともaim？

ambitionは長い間達成したいと思ってきたとても重要な事柄(大志・宿願)を表します。一方、aimは何かをする際に自分が達成したいと思う事柄(目標・目的)を表します。

ex. Sandro's one **ambition** is to play for Italy in the World Cup.
The **aim** of the course is to develop the students' writing skills.

3.「習慣」はcustom、それともhabit？

customは民族やある地域の人々などが長い間行ってきたこと(習慣)を示したり、特定の状況下で人がいつも行うことを示したりします。一方habitは、ある人が繰り返し無意識に行うこと(癖)を表します。

ex. One of their **customs** is to point with the thumb, not with the index finger.
His **custom** of making detailed preparatory drawings makes him unique amongst 18th century British painters.
She has a lot of little **habits** that I find really irritating.

4.「景色」はlandscape、それともscenery？

landscapeは広範囲の陸地、特に田舎を表します。一方sceneryは田舎の、特に特定の場所から眺められる美しい自然の景色(例えば、丘や渓谷、野原など)を表します。

ex. Having reached the top of the hill, we sat and admired the **landscape** that stretched far into the distance.
The train journey takes you through some breathtaking **scenery**.

5.「決めたことは」はchoice、それともdecision？

幅広い可能性の中から望ましいものを選ぶときにはchoiceを用いますが、何かについて、熟慮したあとに判断を下す場合などにはdecisionを用います。

ex. Oxford was my first **choice**, but I didn't get the grades.
Although the job offer is attractive, I'd like more time to make a **decision**.

Unit 8　The Statue of Liberty

6. 日本語になった英語は正しい？

カタカナ英語として日本語になっているものは実際の英語の意味と違っていることがよくあります。例えば、カメラマンはcameramanではなく、photographerを用いますし、エアコンはair-conditioner、サラリーマンはoffice workerと言います。

　　ex.　　　Fish are stored and sold in the plastic **containers**.
　　　　　　I've been looking for **a personal computer**.

7.「聴衆」はaudience、それともcongregation？

audienceは映画や演劇、コンサート、講演などを見たり聞いたりする人のことを示します。一方、congregationは教会の礼拝に参加する人を表します。

　　ex.　　　The group has played to vast **audiences** all over the world.
　　　　　　The minister is always pleased to see new faces in the **congregation**.

8.「機会」はoccasion、それともopportunity？

occasionはある事柄が起こる時期を表します。したがってtimeとほぼ同じ意味になります。一方、opportunityは何かしたいことをすることができる時（時機・機会）を表します。またchanceはopportunityのinformalな表現として用いることもありますが、偶然生じる時機（機会）を示します。

　　ex.　　　I've been to Rome on several **occasions**. (=several times)
　　　　　　The meeting on Tuesday will be a good **opportunity** for you to make some new contacts.

9.「方法」はmethod、それともway？

methodは主に技術的な表現として用いられますが、wayは非技術的な表現として用いられます。また「方法をとる」という場合はadopt a methodという表現を用います。

　　ex.　　　The research project aims to develop new **methods** for trapping solar energy.
　　　　　　There are several **ways** of answering the question.
　　　　　　This new **method** of treating the disease has been widely adopted.

10.「印象、イメージ」はimpression、それともimage？

impressionは短時間の後に誰かまたは何かについて持つ意見や感情を表します。一方imageは自分や自分の会社などについて他人に持ってもらいたいと思っているような一般的な見方を示します。

　　ex.　　　My **impression** is that she would make an excellent teacher.
　　　　　　After all the bad publicity, the company needs to improve its **image**.

Further Study ● 描写をするパラグラフの書き方：人や物を描写する

あるものや人物などを描写するのは言葉を用いて絵をつくり上げるのと同じようなものです。上手に描写をするには正確に、そして詳細に描写していくことが重要です。

ここでは最初の文が話題（topic）となっていて、自由の女神とはどのようなものかという記述が続いています。それぞれの文で自由の女神の詳細が述べられています。

Topic Sentence	I will always remember my first impression of the Statue of Liberty. I was a stranger riding on the ferry across New York Harbor, enjoying the urban landscape and skyline. I remember how small the statue looked in the distance.
Descriptions	"Lady Liberty" is one of the most recognized statues in the world, and is a great American symbol. She is **a 151-foot copper statue** of a woman in classical Roman costume. Her uplraised **right hand holds the "torch of liberty,"** and her **left hand holds a book with the date July 4, 1776 — America's Independence Day**. Upon her head is the **"crown of liberty," with seven spikes representing the seven continents**. The chains under her feet represent liberty crushing the chains of slavery. The statue was **a gift of international friendship from the people of France in 1886 to celebrate American's 100th birthday**. It is now a World Heritage Site.
	The ferry to Liberty Island requires a payment of ten dollars, but admission to the Statue of Liberty itself is free. You can visit the Statue of Liberty museum at the base of the statue. There you can view the original torch, which was replaced in 1984. Visitors used to be able to climb a staircase in the statue to the crown. This was a favorite place for photographers, but was closed after the terrorist attacks of September 11th.
	Over the past 120 years, countless people have sailed past Lady Liberty as they entered New York Harbor. The statue may have looked small to me the first time I saw her, but over the years she has been big enough to hold the dreams of millions of foreigners who came to start new lives in America.

Exercise

● 次の単語リストを使って、どこか自分の記述したい場所を選び87ページのシートにパラグラフを書いてみましょう。

clean	cold	colorful	cool	crowded	dirty	flat
hilly	hot	humid	industrial	modern	mountainous	narrow
old	quiet	rural	sandy	spectacular	wide	windy

Unit 9 Opinion

- 間違いやすい形容詞の使い方 [1]
- 主張を述べるパラグラフの書き方：主張を述べ、展開する

Letter to a Newspaper

Letter
太字の語に注意しながら手紙を読んでみましょう。

Dear Editor:

　In my opinion, smoking should be banned in all restaurants. First of all, there is no reason to subject others to this harmful and dirty habit. Many people find the smell of cigarette smoke to be extremely unpleasant. Secondly, **exhaustive** medical research shows that secondhand smoke is harmful to those nearby. Smokers should be **ashamed** of themselves for exposing others to their addiction.

　In addition, being around secondhand smoke makes food less tasty. For people like me who are more sensitive, there are other health considerations. I have asthma and am extremely allergic to cigarette smoke. Is it fair that I must suffer when I go out to eat?

　I have sympathy for restaurant owners who say that prohibiting smoking will hurt their business, but if you look closely, you see this is not **reasonable**. In major American cities where smoking is banned in restaurants, including New York City, business has actually increased. Perhaps this is because most people are **glad** to eat in a smoke-free environment. Today the number of smokers in **industrial** countries is decreasing, so it's good business to go smoke free.

　However, I realize that restaurant owners do not want to irritate long-time customers who smoke. Perhaps they could set up an outdoor smoking area for those people.

　I am **happy** to know that cigarettes are becoming less acceptable in society. Now is the time for **strict** new laws that ban smoking in restaurants.

Sincerely,
Myron E. Flores

Notes
addiction［中毒］　secondhand smoke［受動喫煙］　asthma［喘息（ぜんそく）］

Practice

A より適切な表現の英文にチェックをつけましょう。

1. ☐ An exhausting investigation finally revealed the cause of the accident.
   ☐ An exhaustive investigation finally revealed the cause of the accident.

2. ☐ One man is able to destroy the whole world.
   ☐ One man is capable of destroying the whole world.

3. ☐ She said she liked the jumper because the color was very peculiar.
   ☐ She said she liked the jumper because the color was very unusual.

4. ☐ Before I actually started to use one, I was suspicious about the value of computers.
   ☐ Before I actually started to use one, I was skeptical about the value of computers.

5. ☐ The teachers are very kind and understanding.
   ☐ The teachers are very kind and comprehensive.

6. ☐ What really made me nervous was the way he kept pulling my sleeve.
   ☐ What really irritated me was the way he kept pulling my sleeve.

7. ☐ The third paragraph of the essay is not relevant.
   ☐ The third paragraph of the essay is not appropriate.

8. ☐ There are severe rules as to what you can wear to school.
   ☐ There are strict rules as to what you can wear to school.

9. ☐ My father's company imports electrical goods.
   ☐ My father's company imports electric goods.

10. ☐ I was far too upset and emotional to make a rational decision.
    ☐ I was far too upset and emotional to make a reasonable decision.

B 誤りがあれば正しい英文に直しましょう。

1. I was interesting to hear she had got married.

2. The South has fewer industrious areas.

3. We hope that you will like this school and be glad here.

4. My actual job involves a lot of administration.

5. If I did the same thing every day, I would be dull.

6. We shall be taking you to see several interesting historical places.

7. My most favorite drink is lemonade.

8. The food was excellent and very tasteful.

9. The belief that Spanish is easy to learn is wrong.

10. I always feel ashamed when I have to speak in public.

C 英語に直しましょう。

1. 彼女がけがをしたかもしれないと思うと、私はとても心配でした。

2. 彼女は明らかにこの仕事に最適な人物です。

3. 銀行での私の仕事はとても退屈でした。

4. 私はポップスよりクラシックのほうが好きです。

5. 彼は私に彼がとったカラー写真を見せてくれました。

Common Errors ● 間違いやすい形容詞の使い方 [1]

1.「疑わしい」はsuspicious、それともskeptical？

suspiciousは誰かが間違ったことをして罪を犯しているのではないかと思えるようなときに用います。一方、skepticalはsceptical（イギリス英語）とも書きますが、人の言っていることを信じていないような場合に用います。

ex. I started to get **suspicious** when he refused to tell me where he had been.
Many doctors remain highly **skeptical** about the value of alternative medicine.

2.「できる」に用いるのはable、それともcapable？

be able toは、あることができるし普通にそのことを行っている場合に用いますが、be capable ofは、普通行わないことだがやろうと思えばやれるという場合に用います。

ex. The doctor said that after a few days I'd be **able** to get out of bed.
I'm sure he's quite **capable** of getting here on time, but he can't be bothered.

3.「間違っている」はwrong、それともmistaken？

wrongは物事が正しくなかったり真実ではない場合に用いますが、mistakenは誤った信念やアイディアに関して述べる場合や、その表現が間違っているときに用います。

ex. I tried to telephone him, but he must have given me the **wrong** number.
Some people have the **mistaken** idea that cats need to drink milk.

4.「厳しい」はsevere、それともstrict？

severeは人が親切でなかったり、友好的でなかったり、ユーモアや共感を示さなかったりする場合や、罰や批判、ダメージに関して述べる場合に用います。一方、strictは常に従うべき法律やルールに関して記述する場合に用います。

ex. Mr. Cameron's angry voice and **severe** expression used to frighten her.
Teachers have to be **strict** or the children take advantage of them.

5.「いらいらする」はnervous、それともirritate？

nervousは自信が持てずに不安だったり、リラックスできないでいる状況に用いる形容詞です。一方irritateは動詞で、誰かをちょっと怒らせていらいらさせたりする場合に用います。このirritateの形容詞としてはirritatedとirritatingを使います。ふたつの違いはinterestedとinterestingの違いと同様です。anxiousは起こるかもしれないことや起こったにちがいないことについてとても心配している場合に用います。

ex. I **hate** the way the teacher watches me when I'm working.
His attempts to sound important **irritate** people.
I couldn't help feeling **anxious**.

6. 「変わっている」はunusual、それともpeculiar？

unusualは普通でない、あるいはまれである場合に用います。一方、peculiarは奇妙であるという意味合いを示し、特に驚いたり不快感を起こさせる状況で用いられます。

ex. At one time it was **unusual** for women to enter politics.
I'm not sure about this cheese. The taste is a bit **peculiar**.

7. 「適切な」はappropriate、suitable、それともrelevant？

appropriateはある特定の状況下で適しているという意味で用います。また、suitableはほぼappropriateと同じ意味で、特に必要な才能や技能などを持っている点で適しているという場合に用います。一方、relevantはやっていることや話していることと関連しているという場合に用います。

ex. To offer them more money at this stage would not be **appropriate**.
The hotel isn't **suitable** for families with children.
You can't enter the country unless you've obtained the **relevant** documents.

8. 「理解力がある」はunderstanding、それともcomprehensive？

understandingは誰かに対して共感を持っている場合に用います。一方、comprehensiveはすべて、あるいはほとんどすべてのことを含むという意味（包括的な）で用います。またcomprehensibleはある事などがわかりやすいという意味で用います。

ex. As people grow older, they tend to be a bit more **understanding**.
The witness provided a **comprehensive** account of the accident.
The object is to make our speech readable and **comprehensible**.

9. 「とても疲れる」はexhausting、exhausted、それともexhaustive？

exhaustingは物事が疲れを引き起こすという場合に用い、exhaustedは人が疲れる場合に用います。一方exhaustiveは細かな部分さえもミスしないくらい徹底的にまたは完璧にすること（「徹底的な、網羅的な」という意味）を表します。

ex. At the end of the day I felt **exhausted**.
Pushing the car was **exhausting**.

10. 「恥ずかしい」はembarrassed、それともashamed？

embarrassedは社会的に居心地悪く感じたり、心配になったりした場合に用います。一方、ashamedはしたことが何か悪いことで自分自身が罪の意識を持っている場合などに用います。

ex. You can imagine how **embarrassed** I felt when I couldn't pay the bill.
Anyone who steals from the poor should be **ashamed** of themselves.

Further Study — 主張を述べるパラグラフの書き方：主張を述べ、展開する

文章を書く場合、しばしば自分が正しいと信じていることについて意見を述べる必要があります。

ここでは、In my opinionという語句によって、話題となる自分の意見を始めています。ほかにtopic sentenceへと導入する語句として使われるものには、I believe (that)、I think (that)、I feel (that)などがあります。パラグラフの中では自分の意見を支持する理由・例・事実などを記述します。そのときよく使われる語句には、First of all、Moreover、For one thing、For example、Also、One reason Is that、Secondly、Thirdly、In addition、Finallyなどがあります。

Topic Sentence

Dear Editor:
　In my opinion, smoking should be banned in all restaurants. **First of all**, there is no reason to subject others to this harmful and dirty habit. Many people find the smell of cigarette smoke to be extremely unpleasant. **Secondly**, exhaustive medical research shows that secondhand smoke is harmful to those nearby. Smokers should be ashamed of themselves for exposing others to their addiction.
　In addition, being around secondhand smoke makes food less tasty. For people like me who are more sensitive, there are other health considerations. I have asthma and am extremely allergic to cigarette smoke. Is it fair that I must suffer when I go out to eat?
　I have sympathy for restaurant owners who say that prohibiting smoking will hurt their business, but if you look closely, you see this is not reasonable. In major American cities where smoking is banned in restaurants, including New York City, business has actually increased. Perhaps this is because most people are glad to eat in a smoke-free environment. Today the number of smokers in industrialized countries is decreasing, so it's good business to go smoke free.
　However, I realize that restaurant owners do not want to irritate long-time customers who smoke. Perhaps they could set up an outdoor smoking area for those people.
I am happy to know that cigarettes are becoming less acceptable in society. Now is the time for strict new laws that ban smoking in restaurants.
Sincerely,
Myron E. Flores

Exercise

A 次のtopic sentencesからトピックを1つ選び、その意見を支持する理由・例・事実などを89ページのリストに箇条書きにまとめてみましょう。

- TV is good for children.
- TV is bad for children.
- ＊＊＊ is a good place to visit.

B 上のリストを利用して、89ページのシートにパラグラフを書いてみましょう。

Unit 10 English Language Newspapers

- 間違いやすい形容詞の使い方 [2]
- 比較と対照を使ったパラグラフの書き方

Different Papers, Different Styles

Passage
太字の語に注意しながら英文を読んでみましょう。

The Times and *The Daily* are just two of the many English language newspapers widely available in countries around the world. Although they have some similarities, these two newspapers also have a number of noteworthy differences.

First, let's compare the two. Both *The Times* and *The Daily* are morning papers published in English in countries in which English is not the native language. Like *The Times*, *The Daily* has sections covering **current** events and **sensitive** political issues as well as news on the economy, TV and radio, and the weather.

Contrasting the two papers, the first thing you'll notice is the difference in price. *The Times* is more **expensive**, while the price of *The Daily* is **lower**. People may buy the **cheaper** newspaper to save money, but in this case, you really get what you pay for.

Because it contains articles from international news services or written originally by native English speakers, *The Times* is more **accurate** in terms of the printed language. *The Daily*, on the other hand, features translated articles from local papers published in their **original** language. Unlike *The Times*, **intense** scrutiny of *The Daily* often reveals **careless** mistakes.

Unlike *The Daily*, *The Times* contains a weekly classified ad section that lists **exciting** job opportunities for **talented** bilingual locals and foreigners. Many who have landed **pleasant** jobs are **thankful** for this **sensible** service.

One excellent feature of *The Daily* makes it a favorite of foreigners **living** overseas. Each day this paper features commentary and world news directly from English-speaking countries. In this way, *The Daily* is really the more international of the two.

Notes
noteworthy [注目すべき]　feature […を特集する]　commentary [論評]

Practice

A より適切な表現の英文にチェックをつけましょう。

1. ☐ The medicine proved very efficient.
   ☐ The medicine proved very effective.

2. ☐ I cannot give you the accurate date of my arrival yet.
   ☐ I cannot give you the exact date of my arrival yet.

3. ☐ If you wish to make a good impression, you'll have to look a bit more respectable.
   ☐ If you wish to make a good impression, you'll have to look a bit more respectful.

4. ☐ Children are very sensible; they all need love and attention.
   ☐ Children are very sensitive; they all need love and attention.

5. ☐ The monthly payments were lower than I'd expected.
   ☐ The monthly payments were cheaper than I'd expected.

6. ☐ How wonderful it would be to be young and carefree again!
   ☐ How wonderful it would be to be young and careless again!

7. ☐ Modern society provides us with material comforts but very few mental rewards.
   ☐ Modern society provides us with material comforts but very few spiritual rewards.

8. ☐ He's a selfish, greedy man and not at all sympathetic.
   ☐ He's a selfish, greedy man and not at all likeable.

9. ☐ I took an intense English conversation course.
   ☐ I took an intensive English conversation course.

10. ☐ We would be very pleasant if you could attend.
    ☐ We would be very pleased if you could attend.

B 誤りがあれば正しい英文に直しましょう。

1. The disadvantage is that the cost is very expensive.

2. It is wonderful to be in London at last. I feel so exciting.

3. I know that Dad will be delightful if you can come.

4. The economical crisis was caused by a sudden increase in the size of the population.

5. The current world encourages creativity.

6. Every alive creature in the sea is affected by pollution.

7. She was wearing an original Japanese "yukata."

8. "You're lucky to have such skillful children," she said.

9. I'm very thankful to you for giving me this opportunity.

10. The city has suffered both natural and artificial disasters.

C 英語に直しましょう。

1. そのリストの名前は(私は)よく知りません(unfamiliar)でした。

2. 戦争のようなある(certain)状況下では食料は配給されなければ(配給する=ration)なりません。

3. 私が明日あなたに会いにいくことは可能(possible)ですか？

4. 泳ぎに行くほうがサッカーをするよりも好ましい(preferable)。

5. 正しい答えは10ページの下で見つけられます。

Common Errors ● 間違いやすい形容詞の使い方 [2]

1.「値段が高い／安い」はexpensive、cheap、high、それともlow？

値段・支払い・賃貸料・給料・収入・支出・料金などが高い／安いなどを言う場合は、highやlowを用います（costs、payments、rents、wages、salaries、incomes、expenses、taxes、feesなど）。商品そのもの自体などの高い／安いは「高価だ」「安価だ」という意味でexpensive、cheapを用います。

ex. During the recession, prices stayed **low**.
Rents in Helsinki are very **high** compared to the rest of Finland.
The jewels are too **expensive** for me to buy.

2.「効果的」はefficient、それともeffective？

efficientは素早くかつ無駄なく機能する場合に用い、「効率がいい」という意味を表します。一方、effectiveは望んでいる効果が見える場合に用い、「効果的な」という意味を表します。

ex. The more **efficient** the engine, the less petrol it uses.
There are many **effective** ways of using computers for training purposes.

3.「才能がある」はskillful、それともtalented？

skillfulは技能を持っていたり技能がしっかりしているという意味で用いますが、talentedは何かをうまく行える生まれながらの能力があることを表します。

ex. Although he lacked Tyson's knock-out punch, he was the more **skillful** of the two boxers.
This **talented** young musician gave his first public performance at the age of five.

4.「経済的」はeconomic、それともeconomical？

economicはある国または地域の経済に関わることに用い、「経済的」という意味を表します。一方、economicalはあるものが他の似通ったものを使うより安上がりであるという状況で用い、「節約になる、徳用の」という意味を表します。

ex. The country's **economic** growth is considered to be too slow.
This house has a very **economical** heating system.

5.「正確な」はaccurate、それともexact？

accurateは発言されたり書かれたりしている内容がまったく間違いのない状況に用いたり、あるものが間違った結果を生み出さない場合（例えば、間違った計測をしない体重計など）、それが正確であるという意味で用いたりします。一方、exactは正確で可能なかぎり詳細に述べられている場合などに用います。

ex. Her novels are always historically **accurate**.
Are you sure the bathroom scales are **accurate**?
The **exact** time is three minutes to seven.

6.「敏感な」はsensible、それともsensitive？

sensibleは道理にかなった決定をする人や、愚かで危険な行動を決してしない人を述べるときに用います。一方、sensitiveは簡単に落胆したり、立腹したりする人を述べるときに用います。

ex. I'm glad to see that she was **sensible** enough to bring some warm clothes.
He's very **sensitive** about his weight, so try not to mention it.

7.「精神的な」はmental、それともspiritual？

mentalは心の中で起こっていたり心理的な影響を与えている場合に用い、「精神の中の、心的な、頭の中で行う」などの意味を表します。一方、spiritualは人間が持つ深い考えや感情の部分に関わる場合に用い、「精神的な、霊的な、魂の」などの意味を表します。

ex. People who have had **mental** illnesses are often unwilling to talk about them.
African music has a **spiritual** quality which is often lacking in Western music.

8.「楽しい」はdelightful、それともdelighted？

delightfulはかなりformalな表現で、(事柄などが)大きな喜びを与える場合に用います。一方、delightedは(人が)非常に喜ばされる場合に用います。

ex. Thank you for such a **delightful** evening.
I'm **delighted** to have finally met her.

9.「集中的」はintense、それともintensive？

intenseは「強い、激しい」という意味合いで使います。一方intensiveは「集中した」という意味で用います。

ex. Pigmentation is more **intense** in the humid tropics than in arid climates.
Intensive agriculture is practiced chiefly where farmland is scarce.

10.「現代」はcurrent、それともmodern？

currentは今起こっていることまたは今存在していることで長く続く可能性がない場合に用います。一方、modernは我々が今生きている、あるいはそんなに昔ではない時代に使われたり存在したりしていたものに対して用います。

ex. How long has she been going out with her **current** boyfriend?
What do you think of **modern** architecture?

Further Study ● 比較と対照を使ったパラグラフの書き方

メインアイディアでは2つの新聞について比較しています。それらの違いをいくつか指摘する形で、メインアイディアを支持する文が構成されています。類似性や違いを示す場合によく使われる語には、both、have ... in common、like、similarly、similar、similar to、the same、likewise、although、however、on the other hand、but、yet、different from、unlike などがあります。

Topic Sentence	*The Times* and *The Daily* are just two of the many English language newspapers widely available in countries around the world. **Although** they have some similarities, these two newspapers also have a number of noteworthy differences.
Supporting Sentences	First, let's compare the two. Both *The Times* and *The Daily* are morning papers published in English in countries in which English is not the native language. **Like** *The Times*, *The Daily* has sections covering current events and sensitive political issues as well as news on the economy, TV and radio, and the weather. **Contrasting** the two papers, the first thing you'll notice is the difference in price. *The Times* is more expensive, **while** the price of *The Daily* is lower. People may buy the cheaper newspaper to save money, **but** in this case, you really get what you pay for. Because it contains articles from international news services or written originally by native English speakers, *The Times* is more accurate in terms of the printed language. *The Daily*, **on the other hand**, features translated articles from local papers published in their original language. **Unlike** *The Times*, intense scrutiny of *The Daily* often reveals careless mistakes. **Unlike** *The Daily*, *The Times* contains a weekly classified ad section that lists exciting job opportunities for talented bilingual locals and foreigners. Many who have landed pleasant jobs are thankful for this sensible service. One excellent feature of *The Daily* makes it a favorite of foreigners living overseas. Each day this paper features commentary and world news directly from English-speaking countries. In this way, *The Daily* is really the more international of the two.

Exercise

A 91ページのAのパラグラフを読んで、比較・対比を示す表現に下線を引いてみましょう。

B 91ページのBのパラグラフを読んで、比較・対比を示す表現に下線を引いてみましょう。

Unit 11　Managing Stress

- 間違いやすい副詞の使い方
- 原因と結果についてのパラグラフの書き方

Your Key to College Success

Passage　太字の語に注意しながら英文を読んでみましょう。

　Students must manage stress in order to be successful in college. Stress can cause sleeplessness, endless worry, and feelings of dread. It **often** prevents people from working effectively and can lead to serious health problems. Stress is a physical, mental and emotional condition that is **usually** fought on several different fronts.

　Physical exercise is an excellent way to relieve stress. It has been said that a body never **completely** in motion can ever be **completely** at rest. Most people **actually** sleep more deeply and awake more refreshed after a physically active day. Jogging, swimming and other strenuous physical activities **definitely** cause the body to make stress-fighting chemicals called endorphins. Listening to relaxing music, meditating, doing yoga, or going for a brisk walk may seem like wasting time **at first**, but can help with stress.

　Another way to control stress is by **effectively** managing your time. Sharon is a busy college student who also works part-time. Every Sunday night she plans her upcoming week. She writes down her class and work schedule, and times for exercise, errands and **especially** social activities. "I **always** schedule time to do the important things, but I also make time to play," she said.

　To be honest, emotional balance is also important for managing stress. Do your best, but remember you're not perfect and don't criticize yourself too much for mistakes. Find ways to focus on something besides your own problems. Reach out to friends when they're feeling down. Volunteer to help those less fortunate than you. Maybe you could tutor children in reading or help handicapped people learn to swim. And make a list of things in your life for which you are grateful.

Notes
dread［恐怖］　strenuous［非常に活発な］　endorphin［エンドルフィン］　meditating［黙想］　brisk walk［きびきび歩くこと］
errand［使い走り］　schedule［予定を立てる］　tutor［教える］

Practice

A より適切な表現の英文にチェックをつけましょう。

1. ☐ She almost couldn't breathe.
   ☐ She could hardly breathe.

2. ☐ The secretary confirmed that there was indeed a young man being held in prison.
   ☐ The secretary confirmed that there was effectively a young man being held in prison.

3. ☐ It was an absolutely terrible flight. The next time I will surely go by train.
   ☐ It was an absolutely terrible flight. The next time I will definitely go by train.

4. ☐ To his great amazement, little Nicola actually won the race.
   ☐ To his great amazement, little Nicola really won the race.

5. ☐ Come to spend the weekend with me. I live always at the same address in L.A.
   ☐ Come to spend the weekend with me. I still live at the same address in L.A.

6. ☐ To be honest, we didn't play very well in the final.
   ☐ Honestly, we didn't play very well in the final.

7. ☐ I am pleased to be able to write to you eventually.
   ☐ I am pleased to be able to write to you at last.

8. ☐ Suddenly the engine started to make a strange noise. Naturally, I stopped the car at once to see what had happened.
   ☐ Suddenly the engine started to make a strange noise. Certainly I stopped the car at once to see what had happened.

9. ☐ I've only been here for two months so far.
   ☐ I've only been here for two months until now.

10. ☐ In Sweden, many wives and husbands stay at home alternately to look after their children.
    ☐ In Sweden, many wives and husbands stay at home alternatively to look after their children.

B 誤りがあれば正しい英文に直しましょう。

1. Society shouldn't punish these people too hardly.

2. I enjoy this type of music still now.

3. Firstly, I couldn't understand the local people at all.

4. Although I am a member of the club, I barely go there.

5. The shop assistant asked me gently what I wanted.

6. He spends them money but scarcely goes to see them.

7. I have to make sure that our customers are utterly satisfied.

8. Ordering a meal can be very difficult, specially when there is no menu.

9. We started going out together as friends. Afterwards we both realized that there was more than just friendship.

C 英語に直しましょう。

1. 私はいつも家族の中で一番早く起きます。

2. 朝は普通、冷たいシャワーを浴びます。

3. なぜ冷たいシャワーを浴びるのかとたいてい聞かれます。

4. ときどきその質問で嫌な気分になります。

5. 心配しなくていいですよ。すぐに嫌なことは忘れる性格ですから。

Common Errors　●間違いやすい副詞の使い方

1.「後に」はafterwards、それともlater on ?

afterwardsはある事が終わるとすぐに次に起こってくるというニュアンスで「後に」という意味を表します。一方、later onは2つの行動や出来事の間にかなりの時間が介在する場合に用います。

　　　ex.　●●●●　　On Saturday morning I went to see Adrian in hospital. **Afterwards** I drove into town to do some shopping.
I couldn't understand why she hadn't answered my letters. **Later on** I discovered that she had moved to a new address.

2.「正直に」はto be honest、それともhonestly ?

honestlyは自分の言っていることが真実であるのを誰かに信じてもらいたい場合に用います。一方to be honestは何かについての本当の感情を誰かに伝えようとする場合に用いられ、そのほかにto tell the truth、in all honestly、frankly、to be frankなどがあります。

　　　ex.　●●●●　　I **honestly** don't mind where we go, as long as we go somewhere.
To be honest, I'll be glad when the children are back at school.

3.「本当に」はreally、それともactually ?

reallyとactuallyは時には交換して使える単語ですが、「奇妙に思われるかもしれないが」という意味が出てきた場合は、actuallyを用い、reallyを用いることはありません。

　　　ex.　●●●●　　She sold the piano for a lot more than it was **actually/really** worth.
Instead of running away as he normally does, he **actually** offered to stay.

4. still、so far、until nowの使い方

stillは「今でもなお」という意味を持ち、nowをあとに付けなくてもよい単語です。またso farは、おそらくこれから未来に向けて続くと考えられることについて話をしているとき、「今まで」という意味で用います。until nowも「今まで」という意味がありますが、未来を示すことはなくnowで示す時点までという意味を表します。

　　　ex.　●●●●　　My sister **still** believes in Santa Claus, but I don't.
So far this week it's hardly stopped raining.

5. often、sometimes、usually、alwaysの違いは？

頻度を表す副詞を頻度順・可能性の順に並べてみる場合、100％の可能性があるのはalways、80％の可能性があるのはusually, generally、60％の可能性があるのはoften, frequently、50％の可能性があるのはsometimes、20％の可能性があるのはoccasionally、10％の可能性があるのはseldom、rarely、そして0％の可能性はneverであると言えます。ただし、これは一般的な規準であり、実際には若干異なることもあります。

6. 「特に」はspecially、それともespecially？

speciallyはある事が特別な目的のためになされたり作られたりしたことを表す場合に用いられます。一方、especiallyは上で述べたこと以外に対して用いたり、話し手の言っている内容が特に本当のことであるという点に注意を向けさせるために使われたりします。

ex. We've come all the way from Frankfurt **specially** to see you.
Paris is always full of tourists, **especially** during the summer vacation.

7. 「かわるがわる」はalternatively、それともalternately？

alternativelyはほかの可能性がある場合を示すときに用いられます。一方、alternatelyは「順番に、次から次へ」という意味で用いられます。

ex. I thought we'd stay home. **Alternatively**, you might like to go for a walk.
The play is **alternately** sad and happy.

8. 「確かに」はsurely、それともdefinitely？

surelyはその真実や自分の言っていることの可能性に対してそれが正しいと強調したいときに用います。surelyはしばしば相手に対して同意を強く求めようとするときにも使います。一方、definitelyはあることについて完全に確信している場合に用います。

ex. **Surely** they should have arrived by now!
This is **definitely** the best film she's ever made.

9. 「完全に」はutterly、それともcompletely？

utterlyは否定的な意味を持った単語や不満・反感を表すような単語とともに使われます。(例えば、ridiculous、absurd、irrelevant、useless、wrong、impossible、confused、amazed、dejected、ruined、reject、detest、destroyなど)

ex. This new can opener is **utterly** useless.
The entire building was **utterly** destroyed.

10. notがなくても否定の意味になる語

notという否定を表す語がなくても、その語自体の意味の中に否定的な意味が含まれているものがあります。例えば、hardly、rarely、scarcely、seldomなどです。また焦点が否定ではなく肯定にあるものの、完全に肯定的な意味にならない語にはbarelyがあります。

ex. I could **hardly** believe my eyes.
The beaver **rarely** harms people.

Further Study ● 原因と結果についてのパラグラフの書き方

ある状況を説明する際、その原因(理由)や効果(結果)を分析することが時折必要となります。よい説明文を書くには、ある状況の効果だけではなく、原因をも合わせて記述しないといけません。

ここでは最初の文が話題(topic)となっていて、そのあとの文はその話題の原因(理由)とその影響(効果)あるいは結果を示しています。原因を導入する単語としては、because、since、due toなどがあり、また効果(結果)を導入する単語としては、so、therefore、as a result、thus、consequentlyなどがあります。

Topic Sentence	<u>Students must manage stress in order to be successful in college.</u> Stress can cause sleeplessness, endless worry, and feelings of dread. It often prevents people from working effectively and can lead to serious health problems. Stress is a physical, mental and emotional condition that is usually fought on several different fronts.
Causes and Effects	Physical exercise is an excellent way to relieve stress. It has been said that a body never completely in motion can ever be completely at rest. Most people actually sleep more deeply and awake more refreshed after a physically active day. Jogging, swimming and other strenuous physical activities definitely cause the body to make stress-fighting chemicals called endorphins. Listening to relaxing music, meditating, doing yoga, or going for a brisk walk may seem like wasting time at first, but can help with stress. Another way to control stress is by effectively managing your time. Sharon is a busy college student who also works part-time. Every Sunday night she plans her upcoming week. She writes down her class and work schedule, and times for exercise, errands and especially social activities. "I always schedule time to do the important things, but I also make time to play," she said. To be honest, emotional balance is also important for managing stress. Do your best, but remember you're not perfect and don't criticize yourself too much for mistakes. Find ways to focus on something besides your own problems. Reach out to friends when they're feeling down. Volunteer to help those less fortunate than you. Maybe you could tutor children in reading or help handicapped people learn to swim. And make a list of things in your life for which you are grateful.

Exercise

A 次のtopic sentencesからトピックを1つ選び、その理由を示すリストを93ページのシートに作成してみましょう。

- reasons I came to this school
- reasons I chose my apartment or bought my house
- reasons I chose this job

B 上のリストを利用して93ページのシートにパラグラフを書いてみましょう。

Unit 12 Writing Personal and Business Letters

- その他の間違いやすい表現
- 私信とビジネス・レターの書き方

Communicating on Paper

Letters
太字の語に注意しながら私信とビジネスレターを読んでみましょう。

Dear Aunt Sadie,

　Thank you very much for the digital tape recorder you gave me for my birthday. It is the perfect study tool for college! I use it often, especially **during** class lectures. **At the moment** I'm using it to review last Friday's biology lecture. Of course, I'll also use it **when listening** to my favorite music.

　I truly appreciate your thoughtful gift. I'll think of you and your kindness every time I use it in the years to come.

Love,
Shelly

Dear Sir or Madam:

　I am writing you **with respect to** an order I placed. I recently ordered a desktop computer from you (I have enclosed a copy of the order). **While opening** the box, I saw there was a huge scratch on the screen. Your customer service representative promised to send a replacement monitor immediately, and a prepaid address label so I could return the defective product to you without charge to me. That was three weeks ago and I have yet to receive the replacement monitor or the label.

　While waiting for the replacement monitor, I decided to install the operating system and included software. Although I am a computer science major in university and am quite familiar with the instructions you included, I tried for three hours **without success** to install this software. This was advertised as the most **up-to-date** system, but **from my point of view** it is not nearly as good as earlier versions.

　I have had **too many** problems with this product and would like to return it for a full refund.

　Thank you for your prompt attention to this matter. I await your earliest response.

Sincerely,
Howard Bupkis

✎ Notes
enclose［同封する］　advertise［宣伝する］　full refund［全額払い戻し］

Practice

A より適切な表現の英文にチェックをつけましょう。

1. ☐ The police did their best to rescue the hostages but in vain.
   ☐ The police did their best to rescue the hostages but without success.

2. ☐ At that moment the door opened.
   ☐ In that moment the door opened.

3. ☐ In my opinion, the war is likely to continue.
   ☐ From my point of view, the war is likely to continue.

4. ☐ The Japanese have a tendency to keep silent while meetings.
   ☐ The Japanese have a tendency to keep silent during meetings.

5. ☐ I noticed that he had had a couple of drinks too much.
   ☐ I noticed that he had had a couple of drinks too many.

6. ☐ The school caters for children up to the age of eleven.
   ☐ The school caters for children until the age of eleven.

7. ☐ Concerning your accommodation, there are several possibilities.
   ☐ With regard to your accommodation, there are several possibilities.

8. ☐ My wife had left the hotel and I no longer needed a double room.
   ☐ My wife had left the hotel and I no more needed a double room.

9. ☐ When hearing that the child had been found, she burst into tears.
   ☐ On hearing that the child had been found, she burst into tears.

10. ☐ Over the last few years, unemployment has been increasing.
    ☐ Since the last few years, unemployment has been increasing.

Unit 12 — Writing Personal and Business Letters

B 誤りがあれば正しい英文に直しましょう。

1. According to me, we should spend more money on education.

2. I've never been able to cook. My sister on the contrary is a wonderful cook.

3. Could you let us know your decision until the end of October?

4. Television also gives us the up-to-date news and information.

5. Ueno Park in central Tokyo is very huge.

6. After the accident, I had to stay in hospital during three months.

7. As usually, he arrived five minutes late.

8. Each week he wrote her three letters, as well as telephoned her.

9. We have to train every day, regardless the weather.

10. As a whole, I am very happy here.

C 英語に直しましょう。

1. それはいいアイディアが満載の面白い雑誌です。

2. 忘れずにそこへ早く着くようにしなさい。さもないと (otherwise) 席を取れません。

3. 言うまでもなく、彼の映画は子どもたちにとても人気があります。

4. 「彼女が到着したらすぐに知らせてください。」と彼は叫びました。

5. 私が歌う必要がないかぎり、あなたと一緒に行きます。

Common Errors ● その他の間違いやすい表現

1.「…に関して」はconcerning、それともwith respect to ?

「…に関して」という意味で新しいトピックを導入するときに用いる語句はwith respect to、regarding、as regards、as far as ... concernedなどであり、concerningは用いません。concerningはフォーマルな表現で、質問あるいはある情報が何に関してかを示す場合に用いられます。

  ex. ●●●● **As far as** food **is concerned**, the college has its own cafeteria.

2.「多すぎる」はtoo many、それともtoo much ?

too manyはものが必要とされる以上にあったり、受け入れられる以上にあった場合に用い、manyのあとにくる名詞は数えられる名詞です。一方too muchの場合はそのあとにくる名詞は数えられない名詞です。

  ex. ●●●● I don't like television — there are **too many** commercials.
       I hope I haven't caused you **too much** trouble.

3.「私の意見では」はfrom my point of view、それともin my opinion ?

from one's point of viewはある状況を判断する際に「特定の立場から見て」という意味で用います。一方in one's opinionはある事柄に関する自分の意見(私的意見)を示す場合に用います。

  ex. ●●●● **From the government's point of view**, a June election would make very good sense.

4.「とても」はveryだけ?

強い意味(strong meaning)が備わっている形容詞に対してはveryやextremelyを使うことはできません。(例えば、boiling、convinced、exhausted、huge、terribleなど。これらの単語の意味を強めたいときにはcompletely、totally、utterly、quiteなどを用います。) 一方、強い意味が備わっていない単語にはveryやextremelyを用います。

  ex. ●●●● By the time I got home I was **completely** exhausted.
       By the time I got home, I was **very** tired.

5.「最新の」はup-to-date、それともlatest ?

up-to-dateは最新の知識、情報、発明をもとにして、その機械等が最新であるときに用いたり、また何かについて人が最新の情報を持っている場合にその人が「最新である」という意味で用いたりします。一方、latestは他のものよりも最近設計されたり、生み出されたり、出版されたりしたものを表すときに用います。

  ex. ●●●● Our computer system is reasonably **up-to-date** but it's not flexible enough.
       The BBC World Service always has the **latest** news.

6.「まで」はuntil、up to、それともby？

untilはtillと同様、通常「時」と関連づけて使われます。また、ある時間まで行動や状態が続いているときにも用いられます。up toは特定の年齢と関連づけて「…まで」という意味を表します。一方、byはある時よりも前に始まった行動が遅くともある時期には終了しているという場合に用いられ、「…までに」という意味を表します。

ex. The shops are open **until** six o'clock on weekdays.
I have to submit my thesis **by** the end of next year.

7.「…するとき」はwhen -ing、それともon -ing？

2つのことが同時に起こっていたり、ある事柄が起こったすぐあとに次の事柄が起こっていることを示すときにはon -ingを用います。when -ingはライティングのときに用いられることがあります。この場合ing形はbe + -ingで生じる現在分詞と考えられます。

ex. **On examining** the suitcase, he noticed that the locks had been tampered with.

8.「そのとき」はin a moment、それともat that moment？

in a momentは「すぐに」(very soon)の意味で用いますが、at that momentは「その特定の時に」という意味を表します。注意しなければならないものとしてat the momentという表現があり、これは「今、今のところ」という意味を表すことです。また、the momentは文頭に置いてas soon asの意味で用いられることがあります。

ex. I'll have to go **in a moment**.
At that moment the car skidded on the ice and went off the road.

9.「一方」はon the contrary、それともon the other hand？

on the contraryは述べられた事柄に対して強く反発し、その反対の事柄が真実であると信じている場合などに、「それどころか」という意味で用います。一方、on the other handは以前の記述とはっきりと対照となる記述を導入するときに「一方」という意味で用いられます。

ex. "Your parents didn't want you to go abroad, did they?" "**On the contrary**, they were all for it."
"These computers are amazingly fast. **On the other hand**, they're very expensive."

10.「全体として」はas a whole、それともon the whole？

as a wholeは、対象を単体としてあるいは1つのものとしてとらえた場合に用います。一方、on the wholeは「一般的に言えば」という意味を表します。

ex. The country **as a whole** is not ready for another election.

Further Study　● 私信とビジネス・レターの書き方

ここではbusiness lettersの書き方について見ていきましょう。ビジネス・レターは私的に出す手紙よりも形式的なものになります。

手紙はinside address、greeting、message、closing、signatureから構成されています。時々inside addressの前にheadingを置くことがあり、headingでは送り主の住所と日付が書かれたりします。

Greeting
Dear Sir or Madam:

Message
　I am writing you with respect to an order I placed. I recently ordered a desktop computer from you (I have enclosed a copy of the order). While opening the box, I saw there was a huge scratch on the screen. Your customer service representative promised to send a replacement monitor immediately, and a prepaid address label so I could return the defective product to you without charge to me. That was three weeks ago and I have yet to receive the replacement monitor or the label.

　While waiting for the replacement monitor, I decided to install the operating system and included software. Although I am a computer science major in university and am quite familiar with the instructions you included, I tried for three hours without success to install this software. This was advertised as the most up-to-date system, but from my point of view it is not nearly as good as earlier versions.

　I have had too many problems with this product and would like to return it for a full refund.

　Thank you for your prompt attention to this matter. I await your earliest response.

Closing
Sincerely,

Signature
Howard Bupkis

Exercise

● 95ページのビジネスレターを読んでみましょう。その中に7つのミスがあります。それぞれのミスを訂正してみましょう。

Unit 1 — Making Friends at College

Exercise   **TASK SHEET**

A

Topic sentence: _____

Supporting sentences: _____

_____

_____

_____

_____

B

_____

_____

_____

_____

_____

_____

_____

_____

_____

_____

_____

Date	Class	No.	Name

Unit 2 — My Frantic Day

Exercise

TASK SHEET

July 23 Wednesday

Time	Activity
8:30 – 9:00	greet new students
9:00 – 10:30	give test to new students
10:30 – 11:30	order new textbooks
11:30 – 12:00	make phone call
12:00 – 1:00	have lunch with teachers
1:00 – 3:00	observe classes
3:00 – 4:00	have welcome party

Date	Class	No.	Name

Unit 3 — Time Is Not Money

TASK SHEET

Exercise

A

1. Things to consider when choosing a university.
   (　) cost　(　) location　(　) quality of education　(　) size

2. Difficult things about living in a foreign country.
   (　) new language　(　) unfamiliar customs
   (　) different money　(　) feeling homesick

B

1. There are four important things to consider when choosing a university.

   _____
   _____
   _____
   _____
   _____

2. There are several difficult things about living in a foreign country.

   _____
   _____
   _____
   _____
   _____

Date	Class	No.	Name

Unit 4　Tokyo Disney Resort

Exercise　　TASK SHEET

A

B

Date	Class	No.	Name

Unit 5 — Overseas Travel

Exercise   TASK SHEET

A

B

Date	Class	No.	Name

Unit 6 — Sugar Blamed for Increased Obesity Worldwide

Exercise TASK SHEET

Best times in the eight km run: The first eight years

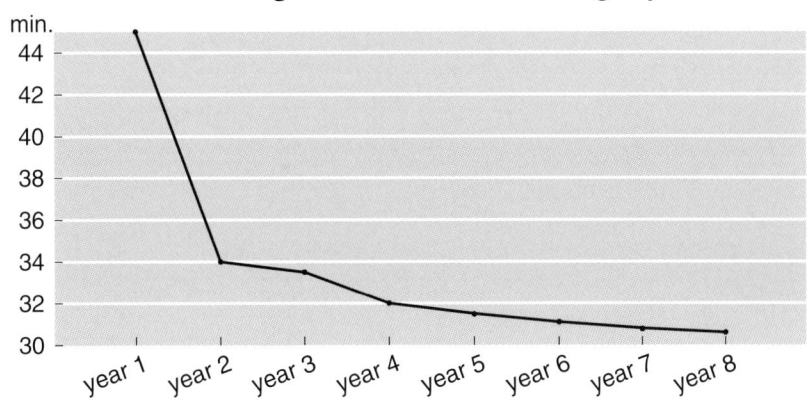

(graph: y-axis min. 30–44, x-axis year 1 – year 8)

1. What is the title of the graph?

2. In which period did the runner make the greatest progress in the eight km run?

3. How long did it take the runner to run eight km at the end of the first year?

4. How long did it take at the end of the second year?

5. What happened during the following six years?

6. What is the difference in time during the first eight year period?

| Date | Class | No. | Name |

Unit 7 — Making the Perfect Cup of Coffee

Exercise **TASK SHEET**

A

Topic sentence: _____

A list of all the steps in the process: _____
_____
_____
_____
_____

B

_____
_____
_____
_____
_____
_____
_____
_____
_____
_____
_____
_____
_____

Date	Class	No.	Name

Unit 8 — The Statue of Liberty

Exercise

TASK SHEET

Date	Class	No.	Name

Unit 9 — Opinion

Exercise — TASK SHEET

A

Topic sentence: _____

Opinion: In my opinion, _____

Reason 1: _____
Reason 2: _____
Reason 3: _____

B

_____
_____
_____
_____
_____
_____
_____
_____
_____
_____
_____

Date	Class	No.	Name

Exercise TASK SHEET

A

The Reporter and *The Monitor* are very similar weekly magazines. First of all, they have many sections in common. For example, both magazines have sections on politics, science, and culture. In addition, both of these popular magazines cost $4.99, and both are read by millions of people around the world. They also have the same cover story almost every week, and they usually review the same books and movies in their culture sections. Another similarity between the two magazines is their point of view. *The Reporter* is very conservative and so is *The Monitor*. Finally, both magazines are translated into ten languages.

B

The Reporter and *Style Magazine* are very different weekly magazines. First of all, they have different sections. *The Reporter* has sections on politics, finance, science and culture. On the other hand, *Style* has sections on fashion, home, decorating, cooking, and gardening. In addition, *The Reporter* costs $3.50 per issue, but *Style* costs $5.00 per issue. Finally, *The Reporter* is translated into ten languages, but *Style* is only in English.

Date	Class	No.	Name

Unit 11 — Managing Stress

Exercise — TASK SHEET

A

Topic sentence:

Reasons:

B

Date	Class	No.	Name

Exercise

TASK SHEET

1123 Greentree Street
Boston, Massachusetts 02766
April 14, 2005

Universal Cosmetic Company
142 Phaidon Place
New York, New York

Dear Sir or Madam:

    I have been using Universal Cosmetic products for many years and I have always been very pleased with it. However, last week I bought a bottle of your newest perfume, Rose Petal, and had terribly results. First, it stained my blouse. It also cause my skin to itch and burn. Worst of all, I couldn't stop sneeze after used it. I feel that this product does not meet your standards of high quality and I would appreciated receiving a refund. I look forward to hearing from you on this matter in the near future.

sincerely,

Mary Johnson
Mary Johnson

Date	Class	No.	Name

本書には CD（別売）があります

Get It Write
コーパス活用英文ライティング入門

2006 年 2 月 1 日　初版第 1 刷発行
2025 年 10 月 15 日　改訂新版第12刷発行

著　者　　市　川　泰　弘
　　　　　Peter Serafin

発行者　　福　岡　正　人
発行所　　株式会社　金　星　堂
（〒101-0051）東京都千代田区神田神保町 3-21
　　　　　　Tel. (03) 3263-3828（営業部）
　　　　　　　　 (03) 3263-3997（編集部）
　　　　　　Fax (03) 3263-0716
　　　　　　https://www.kinsei-do.co.jp

印刷所・製本所／株式会社カシヨ　　　Printed in Japan
本書の無断複製・複写は著作権法上での例外を除き禁じられています。本書を代行業者等の第三者に依頼してスキャンやデジタル化することは、たとえ個人や家庭内での利用であっても認められておりません。
落丁・乱丁本はお取り替えいたします。
ISBN978-4-7647-3988-8　　C1082